the
FREEDOM
OF
MISSING OUT

**LETTING GO OF FEAR
AND SAYING YES TO LIFE**

MICHAEL ROSSMANN, SJ

LOYOLAPRESS.
A JESUIT MINISTRY
Chicago

LOYOLA PRESS.
A JESUIT MINISTRY

www.loyolapress.com

Back cover author photo, Steve Donisch.

ISBN: 978-0-8294-5433-8
Library of Congress Control Number: 2022931998

Printed in the United States of America.
22 23 24 25 26 27 28 29 30 31 Versa 10 9 8 7 6 5 4 3 2 1

*To Mom, who told me to keep my options open
but thankfully didn't follow her own advice.*

Contents

A Roadmap: Freedom, Not Fear

Gulp. I looked at the Gospel passage I would need to preach about: "God made them male and female. . . . They are no longer two but one flesh. Therefore, what God has joined together, no human being must separate." I mean, it's not like there are any land mines when talking about gender, sexuality, marriage, and divorce, right?

A priest does not choose the readings used at church each Sunday. Rather, every Catholic church around the world uses the same readings. There was no getting away from this Gospel passage. I had to pick my poison. Which land mine did I want to step on?

To make things even more interesting, I would not have much time to convey a nuanced message. This was part of the "One-Minute Homily" project. Jesuits give sixty-second video reflections on the Sunday readings and post them on social media—you know, social media, that place where nothing is ever misunderstood and where everyone shows charity!

I decided to sidestep the controversial issues and instead step on a *different* land mine. I discussed what makes many of us just as uncomfortable: commitment. I talked about closing our options and committing to someone or something for life. I argued that the command not to separate what God has joined together is not an arbitrary rule meant to limit our liberty. Rather, it is a proposal for a meaningful life.

I expected a backlash. We are bombarded by messages *not* to settle. Commitment to one thing sounds stagnant, not sexy. I figured this message might not go over well.

The backlash never came. Instead, the response was overwhelmingly positive. It turns out, we're tired and anxious. Commitments might scare us to death, but we also long for something stable. We don't want to stay in a no-man's-land of uncertainty.

There has been much discussion in recent years about the "fear of missing out," or "FOMO." This fear runs deeper than missing out on some party we see on social media. We fear that we will miss out on doing something great with our lives. What if a better option comes around when we're already tied down? We are anxious about making the wrong choice and having to live with it forever. Maybe we worry that we will not follow God's plan for us. We feel overwhelmed when trying to find the best path. We fear having regrets.

We also miss out because of others' choices and the circumstances of life. Our partner breaks up with us. A relative gets deported. The lab report comes back positive. A loved one dies with things left unsaid. Missing out hurts. No wonder people fear it.

Still, this book is about the *freedom* of "missing out" by committing ourselves to something or someone. There is a depth of joy that occurs only when we go all in. A commitment allows us to know where we are going. We can plan for the future. We can enjoy building something great rather than look around to see what might be better. Closing all the other potential doors *sounds* scary. But in reality, it's freeing.

The truth is, we are always missing out. We can never do it all. Saying yes to one path means saying no to many others. Not committing also means missing out. Without commitments, we forgo stability and depth. We have no anchor. If we move all the time, we never have a sense of home. If we run away when a relationship gets tough, we never reach the point of being understood without having to say a word.

If we are busy looking around at all the other possible paths, then we cannot enjoy the person or the situation right in front of us.

I want to be clear: there are situations in which breaking a commitment is the right and healthy thing to do. Abusive relationships, toxic workplaces, and other factors make it necessary sometimes to quit something we thought would be long-term. But this book focuses on the avoidance of commitment that can rob us of true satisfaction and engagement.

While missing out is inevitable, fear is not. The antidote is commitment. Giving up on a quest to find the "best" option allows us to invest ourselves in something and *create* the best option. When we're devoted to a cause, we spend our energy on what matters. It's in serious commitments that we find forgiveness and learn to move on from our mistakes. When we are no longer spread so thin, we can reach greater depth. Without the juggling act of keeping our options open, we can finally let go of the anxiety around making life decisions.

Where We're Going

People told us as kids that we could be anything we want to be. They often did not give us the tools to commit to *something* rather than remain open to *anything*. How do we go about committing to one path and not the thousands of other possibilities? Many of us could use some help.

Part of commitment means saying no. We must say no to many things in order to say yes to something. We prune away many possibilities to embrace some actuality. We close other options to open ourselves to something great.

Sometimes, though, we don't have the choice of saying no. Instead, people say no to *us*. Things don't work out as we planned. We have limitations. There is much that is out of our control. We will find peace only if we learn to accept the many *noes* that life throws our way.

But it's not enough to "just say no" to FOMO and learn to accept the crappy things in life. We also have to be *for* something. The last third of this book will look at how to say yes to something and suck the marrow out of our commitments. When we truly give ourselves to something or someone, much of our anxiety around missing out goes away.

Missing out does not feel pleasant in the short term. We must grieve the closed doors and the paths that are no longer open to us. Still, by accepting the "no"—even embracing the "no"—we can give a wholehearted "yes" to what matters. We experience freedom when we "miss out" by making deep commitments.

Freedom for Good

Perhaps *the* central value in American culture is freedom. Burger King tells us to "have it your way." We can shop online and find just about any conceivable item to purchase. People are free to say what they want, go where they want, and practice whatever religion they want—or none at all. Freedom is great. We rightly celebrate those who have given their lives for us to have it. It's heartbreaking when people do not have the same freedoms we can take for granted.

Still, we often have an underdeveloped notion of what freedom really is. Freedom is more than doing whatever you want without interference. True freedom is the ability to do what is good. It is the adventure of seeking excellence. In *Man's Search for Meaning*, Viktor Frankl argues that freedom always runs the risk of degenerating into arbitrariness without a sense of responsibility. He recommends we supplement the Statue of Liberty on the East Coast with a Statue of Responsibility on the West Coast.[1]

We also run the risk of emphasizing freedom so much that we miss the big picture. Freedom *itself* isn't the point. Rather, freedom allows us to achieve what *is* the point. *New York Times* columnist David Brooks writes, "Freedom isn't an ocean you want to spend your life in. Freedom is a river you want to get across so you can plant yourself on the other side—and fully commit to something."[2] Freedom allows us to do something great with our lives. Having more choices is not the be-all and end-all.

A Life Worth Eulogizing

Brooks makes the distinction between "résumé virtues" and "eulogy virtues."[3] Résumé virtues contribute to professional success. Eulogy virtues are what we talk about at a funeral. Many of us recognize that eulogy virtues are more important but then spend more of our time working on the résumé virtues.

When we eulogize someone who has died, we talk about that person's commitments. No one mentions the thousands of "friends" one had on social media or the TV shows she watched. We talk about her significant relationships. We highlight the impact the deceased had on her community or church. We talk about the career she dedicated herself to for decades.

If we want to do something worth eulogizing, we have to make commitments. Giving a wholehearted "yes" to some things inevitably means saying "no" to other options. We have to reject other possibilities for work to build a meaningful career. Taking marital vows requires more effort than swiping right on a dating app. Committing to a spouse means closing the door to all the other potential partners. We all have many dreams. The great majority of them will need to die to make one or two a reality. Giving a no to many things allows us to give a deeper yes to what really matters.

If we don't commit, our lives feel empty. If we keep things on the surface and fail to invest in any serious way, our lives become an accumulation of experiences without any purpose. If we are pulled in a hundred different directions, then we do not make significant progress in any one direction. Without committing ourselves to particular people and places, we may be doing a lot, but we feel as if we are running in place.

This Isn't Neverland

My grandmother finished school when she was eighteen, got married at the age of twenty, and started having kids soon after. But my generation? It's a different story. One of my brothers started having kids when he was thirty-eight. My other brother and I each started working on yet another degree in our midthirties.

My family is not unique. The average age at marriage has been going up, as has the percentage of people who never get married at all. Other traditional markers of adulthood, such as finishing school, achieving financial independence, and buying a home, are happening later—if at all.

This is not an attack on my generation. Many factors make it harder for young people to break out of the so-called "emerging adulthood" or "extended adolescence." The level of education required for middle-class jobs is higher than in the past. The cost of that education is in a different galaxy. Burdensome student debt prevents many people from buying a place of their own and settling down. The economic downturns of 2008 and 2020 hit young people hard. We don't make it easy for a parent to stay home with a newborn.

But more than economic factors are at play. Sometimes we think we need absolute certainty before we make a big life decision. We think we must have everything in place and *only then* get married or *only then* try out a new endeavor. Something tells me that my grandmother did not have everything in place when she tied the knot at twenty. Those who came before us were figuring things out as they went along—just as we are.

Waiting has consequences. The biological clock is ticking. People who desire children are less likely to conceive the longer they wait. Even for those who are able to have children, it's a lot easier to take care of young kids in one's twenties than in one's forties. Floating through life without serious commitments might be fun, but not achieving the markers of adulthood means missing out on the sense of meaning that comes with them.

We're not Peter Pan. (I know, I know, it's shocking.) We have to grow up. While we cannot control the skyrocketing cost of education, we're often less courageous than we could be. Economic conditions have changed. The need to step forward into the unknown has not. Debt may delay our plans, but cowardice ought not delay them further.

It might be comfortable to imagine that age does not matter and that we can always get around to things later. But that's not helpful. We *can't* delay things forever. A sense of self-worth in adulthood does not come from living like an adolescent.

The Freedom of Structure

I have met some college students who don't want to commit to any activities because they want to focus on school. They have no job. They're not involved in clubs. They do not attend religious gatherings. They are there to concentrate on *college*.

Such students often do not perform well in school. With all the time in the world, there's little pressure to write that paper or study for that exam. There's no structure, nothing to latch on to. The hazy mass of time gets filled up with some combination of video games, social media, sleep, and alcohol.

The students who have a reasonable number of commitments tend to do the best. When I was in college, it always seemed like the female rowers were the top students. The discipline needed to wake up at dawn to train on the water seemed to transfer to the other parts of their lives.

Data illustrate this dynamic. The Bureau of Labor Statistics found that college students who work more than twenty hours a week have a lower average GPA than students who work under twenty hours a week.[4] This makes sense. Working more than twenty hours a week while also being a full-time student is a lot. We have limits. We cannot do it all. The more interesting finding was that students who worked about ten hours per week outperformed students who did not have a job at all. Students without a job may have had more time, yet they often weren't as organized as students who had a job. A lack of commitment can lead to a lack of structure. This can hinder our flourishing.

The Walls of a Playground

When one thinks of Catholic doctrine, freedom is probably not the first thing that comes to mind. People might picture the stereotypical ruler-wielding nun or the discomfort felt in confessing one's sins to a priest. A whole bunch of "thou shalt nots" would seem to limit one's liberty.

Still, in his classic *Orthodoxy*, G. K. Chesterton compares Catholic doctrine and discipline to the walls of a playground near the edge of a cliff. If there is a wall around the playground, children can play freely. Without walls, there is no play. Absolute caution is necessary. With a fear of falling, joy ceases. Only with some guardrails can people have freedom to move around and enjoy themselves. Chesterton continues,

> The unpopular parts of Christianity turn out when examined to be the very props of the people. The outer ring of Christianity is a rigid guard of ethical abnegations and professional priests; but inside that inhuman guard you will find the old human life dancing like children and drinking wine like men.[5]

As a Catholic priest—and a fan of dancing and wine!—it's no surprise that I think Chesterton is onto something. Still, many of the dynamics that Chesterton describes are not unique to Christianity. Total freedom leaves us floundering. We need collective wisdom. We need direction. We need something to orient our lives.

A religious person must follow a set of teachings but can also take deep comfort in being part of an ancient tradition and supportive community. The professional musician must dedicate countless hours to practice but can then dazzle others with her music. Parents of young children rarely get a break—and it doesn't exactly get easier during the teenage years. Still, bringing other humans into this world and raising them to become good people is an exercise in meaning. Committing to something larger than oneself does not erase who we are. Commitments draw out our potential. They make life richer.

But that may not be evident to the uncommitted person. Getting up every Sunday morning to go to church rather than sleeping in or eating brunch seems like a burden. Practicing one's instrument for hours a day sounds like a lot of work. To the person who enjoys traveling on a whim and having time to oneself, a child could seem like a ball and chain. To the uncommitted person, going "all in" would seem to limit one's options. And we fear missing out. It's not surprising that we often fail to commit.

Whatever Is Excellent

I find freedom in my commitment to be a Catholic priest. I appreciate a tradition that includes saints who were far wiser and holier than I am. Still, I don't need to miss out on wisdom from non-Christian or nonreligious sources. In fact, many of the people I read, watch, and listen to are not religious. Most of the insights of this book are not unique to Christianity. I will take an approach reflected in one of my favorite lines in Scripture:

> Whatever is true, whatever is honorable, whatever is just, whatever is pure, whatever is pleasing, whatever is commendable, if there is any excellence and if there is anything worthy of praise, think about these things. (Philippians 4:8)

The problem of saying no is not unique to Christians. The experience of freedom that comes from deep commitment is also not distinctively Christian. While I'm not going to hide my Catholicism, I hope what I say will be accessible to people of all faith backgrounds or no faith background. We're in this together.

What Can I Do Now?

Ultimately, the only way to achieve meaning and a sense of importance in one's life is through a rejection of alternatives, a narrowing of freedom, a choice of commitment to one place, one belief, or (gulp) one person.[6]

—Mark Manson

When has fear prevented me from making commitments?

When have I felt overwhelmed by my freedom to choose among many options?

Can I identify a situation in which I experienced relief after going all-in with a commitment?

Can I identify a situation in which I stopped searching for the "best" option to commit to something and *create* the best option?

SAYING NO

1

It's Not Always Wise to "Keep Your Options Open"

For most of human existence, missing out meant *missing out*. Not participating in the hunt or the harvest could mean starvation. Not getting married or having children could result in having no one to take care of you. Not practicing the customs of one's tribe or town could mean social isolation. It's no wonder we fear missing out.

It's also not surprising that we struggle to say no. We are wealthier than 99.9 percent of humans in history. There were far fewer options for our ancestors. If everyone in your village is a farmer, then you don't need to spend much time deciding what to do for a living. We have more opportunities than those who came before us—and more anxiety about choosing the wrong path. When life was "nasty, brutish, and short," in the words of Thomas Hobbes, most people struggled to get by.[7] Dealing with nearly limitless options is a rather new human phenomenon.

Having some options is a wonderful thing. Most of us enjoy being able to choose what to do for a living or whom to marry. No one wants to go back to the days of three television stations—or no television stations! In choosing what to buy, we've gotten past the era when Henry Ford said that you could have a car "painted any color . . . so long as it is black." No one is hoping to go back to the time when life was "nasty, brutish, and short." In a state of deprivation, more freedom is a good thing.

Still, that does not mean that more choice is always good. Think of your favorite restaurant. Would tripling the size of their menu make it better? If it's a pizza place, should they also offer burritos and sushi? The more the restaurant tries to offer, the less likely it is to be great at any one thing. A jack-of-all-trades is a master of none.

Enough with the Options!

At a certain point, adding more choices is not helpful. I love a hoppy IPA. Almost any bar in the United States is going to have at least one. They often have more. Sometimes *many* more.

But here's the thing: I love *a* good IPA. I don't need to choose from a beer list that spans multiple pages. It's nice to have some choice, but it's overwhelming to choose from among too many options.

The more options we have, the more options we do not choose—and the greater the opportunity for regret. I enjoy a Bell's Two Hearted Ale less when thinking, "Should I have ordered a Lagunitas or Sierra Nevada instead?" It's great to have some options. It's stressful to have too many.

Sheena Iyengar of Columbia Business School conducted a famous experiment in the psychology of choice.[8] She and her colleagues set up a tasting booth near the entrance of an upscale grocery store and offered free samples of jam. Half the time, they had six jams that people could sample. For the other half, they had twenty-four different jams.

We like the idea of having many options. Sure enough, the more jam options there were, the more likely people were to stop by the tasting booth. When there were twenty-four jams, 60 percent of people stopped at the table. When there were six jams, only 40 percent of shoppers sampled some jam.

Still, while we're drawn to options, it's difficult to deal with too many of them. When there were six options, a full 30 percent of those who stopped by the table went on to buy some jam. When there were twenty-four jams, only *three* percent purchased any jam. We might tell ourselves, "I've always liked raspberry, but maybe I should get blueberry-pomegranate. Or what about strawberry-mango? This is stressful! I think I'll buy some wine instead." Having too many options disorients us. We struggle to make forward progress.

Some companies have noticed how customers are overwhelmed. Reducing options can also increase the company's bottom line. While a Walmart supercenter stocks more than 100,000 different items, the grocery store Aldi stocks fewer than 1,500.[9] Having fewer options reduces the shoppers' mental fatigue and Aldi's cost to stock so many different items.

The British supermarket chain Tesco noticed that stores like Aldi were eating into their market share. A shopper at Aldi has one type of ketchup to choose from. If a man's wife sends him to get ketchup at the store, he knows exactly what to buy. At Tesco? There were twenty-eight different types of ketchup. That simple errand became a stressful experience: *Which of the twenty-eight options does my wife want?* Now multiply that experience by every item on the shopping list. Tesco decided to remove 30,000 of the 90,000 items it stocked to reduce the shoppers' anxiety and increase the company's profits.[10] Sometimes less is more.

Keep Your Options Closed

Advice often has an expiration date. What's helpful at one time can be misguided at a different time. "Keep your options open" is one of those sayings with a limited shelf life.

We have probably all heard people tell us to keep our options open. It sounds reasonable. We can think of times we rushed into something too quickly and then regretted it later. And, come on, who doesn't like *options*?

But taken too far, "keep your options open" is terrible advice. The problem occurs when we keep our options open for so long that we never commit to anyone or anything. The uncommitted person is the unremarkable person.

Now, at the beginning of college, it is helpful to keep one's options open. We should not expect eighteen-year-olds to know exactly what to do for the rest of their lives. We need a variety of experiences to know what makes us come alive and how best we can cultivate and share our gifts. We need to dip our toes in the water before we dive in headfirst.

Even if a young person has a career plan, there's still no need to get locked into a certain track without any room to explore other interests. Perhaps a young woman plans on being a medical doctor but wants to take an anthropology course. Great! Go for it. It can be helpful to bring a range of experiences and interests to our various commitments.

Even for those of us who are not exactly young *in age* but are young *at heart*, it can often be wise to take a keep-your-options-open stance. The weather may affect one's weekend plans to be outdoors. There may not be a place available in the neighborhood where one wants to live. It can be good to have a backup option.

Life also intervenes. A death occurs. A global pandemic arises. An accident happens. We have to adapt. Whether we like it or not, we must figure out other options.

But here's the thing: most young people—and most not-so-young people—don't struggle with keeping their options open. Most of us are *experts* at keeping our options open. Most of us struggle to commit to something or someone and do it for the long haul. We keep things on the surface in a relationship because someone better might come along. We even struggle to commit to weekend plans.

Openness Has Consequences

Keeping our options open has consequences. During all the time we're keeping our options open, we're missing out on building something great. We can flounder for years—even decades—while keeping our options open.

Warren Buffett advises people to start doing what they truly want rather than wait for years as they keep their options open. He once met a student at Harvard Business School who listed his accomplishments and said, "I thought it would really round out my résumé perfectly if I went to work now for a big management consulting firm."

Buffett responded, "Well, is that what you want to do?"

The young man said, "No, but that's the perfect résumé."

Buffett asked, "When are you going to start doing what you like?"

The Harvard student said, "Well, I'll get to that someday."

Buffett responded, "Well, you know, your plan sounds to me a lot like saving up sex for your old age. It just doesn't make a lot of sense."[11]

It's reasonable to prioritize flexibility early in life. It's wise to develop skills that are going to be valuable in any workplace. But life is short. Sooner rather than later, we need to find something good and give ourselves to it. Being miserable for decades as we prepare for some supposedly perfect future is not worth it.

Getting Stuck in Optionality

Sometimes we get stuck in an option-maximization cycle. We focus on *acquiring* options and forget that we need to *realize* a few options if we want to do something meaningful with our lives.

Mihir Desai, a professor at Harvard Business School and Harvard Law School, has noticed how this effort to acquire options can backfire. He writes, "Instead of enabling young people to take on risks and make choices, acquiring options becomes habitual. You can never create enough option value—and the longer you spend acquiring options, the harder it is to stop."[12]

Rather than create confidence to do something bold, options can become a drug. We want more. Desai notes that he has seen many of his former students never get around to realizing their dreams of becoming entrepreneurs or artists. They plan on working as consultants or getting their MBA as a safety net before doing what they want to do. Instead, Desai writes, "These safety nets don't end up enabling big risk-taking—individuals just become habitual acquirers of safety nets."[13]

It's helpful to have *a* backup plan, but there's a danger in acquiring so many backup plans that we never commit to anything. People will remember us for our actual commitments, not a list of potential options. Our lives are better when we invest in actuality, not optionality.

The keep-your-options-open mindset can also affect the commitments we do make. Barry Schwartz writes in *The Paradox of Choice*, "As we see reversible marriages come apart, we may think to ourselves, how fortunate the couple was to have a flexible attitude toward marital commitment, given that it didn't work out. It might not occur to us that the flexible attitude might have played a causal role in the marriage's failure."[14] The temptation to never *really* commit sets us up for dissatisfaction. If we're questioning whether this thing or person is "the best," we can miss out on seeing something great right in front of us. If our commitments are tepid, unhappiness creeps in.

Getting Off the Upgrade Treadmill

When buying a phone, we know that it will not last for life. Phones break. They slow down. Phone companies release new versions all the time. Even if a phone is working fine, we often feel the itch to upgrade to a better phone after a couple of years. If most people around us have a device that is much better than ours, it is difficult to resist the urge to follow the crowd. While this can lead to landfills brimming with our old devices, upgrading our technology is a significant part of the human story. We've come a long way since the time of stone tools. The urge to upgrade has led to astonishing technological development and material success.

As beneficial as this upgrade mentality has been for our material well-being, it can be disastrous if we transfer it to our personal lives. The most important parts of life are not like a technology upgrade. We don't ditch a life partner because a new "product" is on the market. We don't trade in a child because we discover a particular "bug" in his or her operating system. The only way to have some peace in life is to get off the upgrade treadmill and make commitments. At a certain point, we must close our options and throw in our lot with particular people, institutions, and communities—bugs and all. When trade-ins aren't an option, we can then invest in what we have. Deep commitment leads to the best upgrade.

Does this mean that we should *never* quit a serious commitment? Of course not. For example, one should not be expected to stay in an abusive relationship. In their pastoral document "When I Call for Help," the U.S. Catholic bishops write that acting to end abuse does not violate marital vows. In such a situation, it's violence and abuse, not divorce, that break up the marriage.[15]

What about quitting something like a toxic workplace? It may be physically safe but still a significant drag on one's well-being. There's no till-death-do-us-part commitment to an employer, but leaving a job is a big decision. St. Ignatius's advice could prove helpful. In his "Rules for Discernment," he notes that one should not make a change when one is currently experiencing desolation. Quitting might be the right thing, but not when we are in a rage. We should wait until we're personally in a good place to make a significant change.

"Freedom" to Change

In one of the most popular TED talks of all time, Daniel Gilbert of Harvard illustrates how keeping your options open can be a happiness killer.[16] He and Jane Ebert crafted an experiment in which they invited students to participate in a photography course and learn how to use a darkroom. The students created beautiful 8 x 10 glossies of their two favorite pictures. They were then told that they could keep only one of their two photos. They had to choose.

They divided participants into two groups. They told some students that they had to make an irreversible decision about which photo to keep. They told other students that if they changed their mind about which photograph they wanted, they could swap it out over the next four days.

The results were surprising. Students without the option to change their picture were happy with what they chose. Those with the option of swapping their photo were not so happy. They agonized over their decision: *Did I choose the right one?* This deliberation wrecked their satisfaction. Even after the window of time when they could change photos was closed, they still did not like their picture. Rather than be content with what they had, they found that the "freedom" to change their minds was anything but freeing.

Hearts Broken but Beating

If there's one piece of advice I remember my mother telling me when I was growing up, it's "keep your options open." I am grateful that I never felt the pressure to figure out my future career when I was still figuring out who I was. That being said, I don't think the priesthood was one of the options she had in mind! It took some time for her to accept that.

Still, as often as she told me to keep my options open—and, frankly, she still tells me this—she is not exactly a woman who followed her own advice. And thank God! I'm around today because she closed her options and married my father.

When I was two years old, my dad died of cancer. My mother was left to raise three sons on her own. She didn't see raising my brothers and me as an "option." She put one foot in front of the other and doubled down on her commitment to care for us. She could not bring back my father, but she focused on what she could control. And she did *marvelously*.

It was not the experience of family life that my mother anticipated when she got married, but there has been no shortage of love and meaning.

An uncommitted person could look at a situation like my mother's and think *I don't want to be hurt like that.* Death is heartbreaking, and it is but one of many painful possibilities when giving ourselves to others. There is no shortage of songs outlining the pains that are possible when we open our hearts to another. But what's the alternative? Not loving?

We could keep things on the surface. We could keep our options open so that we never commit to someone or something. We could do all that we can to protect our hearts from breaking, but in the process, we also prevent them from fully beating. A life of meaning requires deep commitment. We close our options to open ourselves up to something great.

What Can I Do Now?

To love at all is to be vulnerable. Love anything, and your heart will certainly be wrung and possibly be broken. If you want to make sure of keeping it intact, you must give your heart to no one, not even to an animal. Wrap it carefully round with hobbies and little luxuries; avoid all entanglements; lock it up safe in the casket or coffin of your selfishness. But in that casket—safe, dark, motionless, airless—it will change. It will not be broken; it will become unbreakable, impenetrable, irredeemable.[17]

—C. S. Lewis

Which is worse: committing to another and having that person break your heart, or never giving your heart away at all?

Have I ever "committed" while keeping my options open—thus, not really committing? If so, what were the consequences?

Have I ever experienced freedom by *closing* my options and saying yes to someone or something? If so, what happened then?

When have I found joy in stepping off the "upgrade treadmill"? Or, if I haven't, what has prevented me from it?

2

The Power of Pruning

Mike Flint, the personal pilot for Warren Buffett, was once talking with his boss about his career ambitions. Buffett advised Flint to list his top twenty-five career goals. After Flint made a list of his goals, Buffett told him to circle his top five goals from that list.

And here's where things got interesting. "Everything you didn't circle just became your avoid-at-all-cost list," said Buffett. "No matter what, these things get no attention from you until you've succeeded with your top five."[18]

Think of how painful this would be to practice. Most of us can come up with more than five goals for our future careers. Buffett isn't advising someone to get rid of only the goals that are silly or impractical. He's advising someone to avoid all but the cream of the crop. That means saying no to many good options and focusing only on the best options.

Of course, this advice is coming from one of the richest men on earth. At the time of this writing, Buffett has a net worth of more than $100 billion. He may know a thing or two about career success. Buffett has seen people's good options prevent them from realizing their best options. His advice to focus on what is most important is relevant not only for business success.

Prune to Grow

Few things bring me as much joy as maintaining a garden. Nothing beats the experience of biting into a just-picked garden tomato. Collaborating with creation is fascinating and satisfying. I often have a spring in my step after spending time in the garden.

There is one thing about gardening that I hate: pruning. I hate removing unproductive branches. It pains me to thin seedlings. They have just germinated. I was the one who put them there. And then I have to snuff out their life? It feels so *cruel*. Why can't everything grow?

But every gardener knows that it doesn't work like that. If I do not remove young branches, then adequate nutrients will not reach the older parts that produce fruit. If plants are growing too close together, their root systems will compete over the same space. Trying to grow too many plants will produce less than if fewer plants are grown in the same area.

This is hard for me to accept. Even though a seed packet tells you exactly how much space there should be between plants, I resist. I think, *But maybe the seed packet is lying! Maybe my soil is magically more nutrient rich than all other soils* (despite abundant evidence to the contrary). I thus make the same mistake of planting seeds too close together and failing to prune.

The need for pruning extends beyond the garden. There's not space for every plant, and there's not time to accomplish everything we would like to do. We need to prioritize. We have new ideas and goals, and many of these "sprouts" may be very good. But there is not enough time to act on them all. Our mental and emotional "nutrients" are limited. Pruning the nonessential can allow for growth in what matters.

I am not the first to talk about the need for pruning in our lives. It's an image that Christ used in his teaching: "I am the true vine, and my Father is the vine grower. He removes every branch in me that does not bear fruit. Every branch that bears fruit he prunes to make it bear more fruit" (John 15:1–2). We need to remove the nonessential to give ourselves to that which really matters. We ought to ask ourselves, *What's most important? What's good but doesn't make the cut?*

Opportunity Costs

In college, I was a double major in theology and economics. If the God thing didn't work out, I could always fall back on mammon. While God won, economics shaped my thinking, especially the idea of the opportunity cost—the "cost" of not enjoying the next-best alternative. For example, if I go to an ice cream shop and choose chocolate, the opportunity cost is the enjoyment of vanilla.

In life, there is *always* an opportunity cost. If I stay up and watch a basketball game—something I love—that means that I miss out on a full night of sleep—something else that I love. Becoming a priest meant that I missed out on having a family of my own. Having a family is a wonderful thing. While I am willing to pay the cost of not having a family to follow this vocation that I feel called to, it is a real cost. We simply cannot do everything we would love to do.

The concept of the opportunity cost is helpful for those of us who struggle to say no. If someone asks me to do something, I *hate* saying no. I know I need to. I celebrate when I do say no. But my experience of saying no is like that old arcade game Whac-A-Mole. Requests keep coming. Every time I say no to something, I often find myself saying yes to two more requests that come my way. I grudgingly say yes because I don't want others to see me as a bad person. I tell myself that I'm a priest, that I *should* do this and that. I often "should" all over myself and do not have the time and space to make the most significant impact that I could.

This "should-ing" is not unique to the priesthood. People can tell themselves that they ought to do something because they are a mother or a son or a Christian. While there are some things we should do to be decent human beings, we need to be vigilant that the little *shoulds* we tell ourselves do not distract us from what's important. Warren Buffett says, "The difference between successful people and really successful people is that really successful people say no to almost everything."[19] We cannot do it all.

Buffett's advice echoes another highly successful businessman. Steve Jobs once said in an interview, "People think focus means saying yes to the thing you've got to focus on. But that's not what it means at all. It means saying no to the hundred other good ideas that there are."[20] While the idea of saying no to hundreds of good ideas makes me shudder, I take his point. Jobs knew a thing or two about success.

The next time someone asks you to do something, ask yourself, *If I say yes to this, what am I saying no to?* There is always an opportunity cost. A new commitment reduces the time and energy we have for our previous commitments. We do not get an extra hour in the day if we take on a new project. Something will have to go. To have something positive to bring, we can't be run ragged. If we say yes, we better be prepared to say no.

We're Not Kids Anymore

Pruning is going to look different for each person. A gardener knows to plant more seeds than the number of plants that will be able to grow. Some seeds will never germinate. Some plants experience stunted growth. Some will look tasty to a rabbit and will get eaten before they have a chance to thrive. A gardener does not know from the beginning which will flourish. Instead, she waits and sees which plants are doing well and have the best chance for further growth. And *then* she prunes.

We also need to take some time before we know what to prune from our own lives. A child might need to sample several instruments or activities before finding one or two that really interest her. Many professional athletes did not specialize in a single sport when they were kids. A child may know what he wants to do for the rest of his life, but that's rather rare. Otherwise, we would have many more firefighters! It's normal to scatter many seeds as a child and see what might grow.

Things are different for adults. My dream as a seven-year-old was to play in the NBA. I hope that friends and family would orchestrate an intervention if my 37-year-old self said that he wanted to play in the NBA. That's not going to happen. Still, pruning away that dream of playing in the NBA does not mean I have to eliminate all interest in basketball. I can still be a fan. I can still watch some games during my leisure time. Someone who realizes she's never going to make it as a professional musician can sing in the church choir or play music in the family living room. It's not all or nothing. Still, it is important not to confuse the center and the periphery. We can have hobbies while recognizing that there is a limited amount of time for a few significant life goals.

The need for pruning has taken on a new level of importance in our digital age. We walk around with devices in our pockets that contain more information than the Library of Alexandria. Additionally, the Library of Alexandria did not send push notifications throughout the day. It did not adapt to our preferences and show us what's most likely to make us go down the rabbit hole of social media. We could waste hours watching video after video that YouTube queues up based on our past viewing history. Many of us do.

In the land of the blind, the one-eyed man is king. In a world where everyone is drowning in information, it is those who can filter out the noise who are the kings and queens. This does not mean ditching our devices and living in a cave, but it does mean regular time away from our devices. It means some limits on notifications. It includes an ongoing assessment of what programs are helping us achieve our goals—and which ones are getting in the way.

Social media platforms will always send more content to our feeds. An online video service will suggest another video—or just start playing the next one without asking us to click a thing. It will never suggest that we go outside or call a loved one. Tech CEOs, knowing how addictive their devices are, have often been strict about their own children's technology use. Steve Jobs famously did not allow his kids to use an iPad.[21] Still, the tech titans' *products* do not ask you, "Don't you think you've had enough?" We must swim against the current and say, "No more!" In our contemporary situation of digital abundance, the ability to prune away the nonessential is a superpower.

Winners Often Quit

There has been much discussion about the concept of "grit" in recent years. Angela Duckworth's book *Grit: The Power of Passion and Perseverance* became a bestseller. Duckworth argues that when it comes to success, talent matters, but effort matters more. It is those with stick-to-itiveness who tend to succeed in the long run.[22]

Duckworth's research on endurance is important, but some of the discussion around "grit" misses how the ability to quit is also crucial. All the grit in the world will not allow us to achieve everything that might be of interest to us. We still have to choose what to commit to and what to leave aside. The most successful people give up on many *good* things to do something *great*. They quit many interesting projects so that they have the time and energy to be gritty about what matters. If I try to do everything, I'll never achieve mastery in anything. We can't have "grit" without "quit" if we want to do something great.

People who study productivity note that many of our activities fail to make much of a difference. Checking email for the fifty-seventh time today is not going to move the needle. Blocking out a few hours for deep work without distractions can be a game changer. Morten Hansen of the University of California, Berkeley, notes that top performers "do less, then obsess."[23] They throw themselves into what's going to make a difference and stop wasting their time on what is nonessential. They are gritty about what is important but "quitty" about what is not.

But quitting rubs many of us the wrong way. We grew up hearing "Winners never quit." We watch movies about people who overcame great challenges. We read stories about those who keep at something and beat the odds. A book called *Quit* would likely sell fewer copies than Duckworth's *Grit*.

The fact is, winners quit all the time. They recognize their limitations. They stop going down paths that lead nowhere. They cultivate their God-given gifts. They do not waste time on unproductive activities for which they have no opportunity for success.

You *Can't* Be Anything You Want to Be

One of the sports teams at my high school made a T-shirt that said, "Shoot for the moon. Even if you miss, you'll land among the stars." I hated that T-shirt. It was so saccharine that it made me want to vomit Hallmark cards. Plus, it's wrong. If you shoot for the moon and miss, you're more likely to land among the satellites and be taunted by how far away the stars are.

We tell children that they can be anything they want to be. But *that's not true*! Most of us are not going to make it as supermodels. The odds of a man under six feet tall making it to the NBA are one in two million. If someone is under five feet tall, he'd better find another dream. A man that height has never made it as a professional basketball player. But for those over seven feet? The odds of making it to the NBA are one in seven.[24] Still, those seven-footers better not waste their time dreaming of becoming Olympic gymnasts. It ain't going to happen.

It's normal for children to dream of becoming superheroes and unicorns and all sorts of things they cannot become. But we need to grow up. Problems arise when we continue thinking that we can be anything we want to be. We find freedom when we accept our limitations.

We're better off focusing on the areas where we can thrive and where we can put our gifts to the service of others. Thomas Jefferson was a terrible public speaker. He even faked illnesses to avoid giving speeches. He knew his limitations—and his gifts. He focused on writing, and we have the Declaration of Independence to show for it.

We can't be anything. And that's okay. We can still be something. There are areas where each one of us can excel. We will be happier pursuing what is attainable rather than spinning our wheels while failing at something we're never going to accomplish.

Freedom in Limitation

Daniel Gilbert invites people to contemplate two different futures and think about which they might prefer: winning the lottery or becoming a paraplegic. It sounds absurd. Who would not want to win the lottery? Who on earth would want to become a paraplegic? According to Gilbert's research, however, lottery winners and paraplegics are equally happy with their lives a year after either winning the lottery or losing the use of their legs.[25] The ecstasy of winning the lottery fades after a while. The trauma of losing one's limbs lessens over time. A paraplegic cannot but accept his limitations.

While our particular limitations vary, we all have them. Essential to our own sense of freedom is accepting what we cannot control. And it's often those who have endured trying circumstances who have a lot to teach us.

Cardinal Francis George contracted polio at the age of thirteen. He discovered from his experience of physical paralysis "that true freedom is found in coming to terms with limitations, not in imagining that the whole world is going to dispose itself to your will or desires."[26] The high school seminary in Chicago rejected him because of his disability. Fortunately, he was able to attend a different seminary. Years later, he returned as the cardinal archbishop of Chicago. (I wonder what those who rejected him thought.)

While Cardinal George was able to persevere in becoming a priest and bishop, he understood that our desires do not determine the world. A child must learn to live with limitations if he or she is going to succeed in adulthood. We cannot do it all. We all have limitations. Some are more aware of those limitations than others.

In his modern classic *Interior Freedom*, Fr. Jacques Philippe writes,

> To achieve true interior freedom we must train ourselves to accept, peacefully and willingly, plenty of things that seem to contradict our freedom. This means consenting to our personal limitations, our weaknesses, our powerlessness, this or that situation that life imposes on us, and so on. . . . *The situations that really make us grow are precisely those that we do not control.*[27]

We know this in our bones. Freedom comes not by running away from our limitations but by accepting them. A car accident, a partner's infidelity, or a cancer diagnosis are things over which we have little or no control. They may not be our *fault*, but that's beside the point. Whether they are our fault or not, we have the responsibility to respond as best we can. We can control only how we will move forward.

We cannot achieve many of our dreams. There is much that is out of our control. But we can still do something. We can prune away that which is never going to happen to give ourselves to the thing or two that might. We can accept our limitations and flourish where we can.

What Can I Do Now?

Quitting, done for the right reason, is not giving up. It's not submitting or throwing in the towel. It is saying that a job just doesn't suit us. It is trying something and not liking it. In this way, quitting is actually part of the process of discovery. We define who we are by quitting, whether it's a club, school, job, or hobby. Forced adherence or unquestioned devotion leads to atrophy—to slowly dying. But quitting is the process of growing, the process of living.[28]

—Rich Karlgaard

What activities are deserving of my grit?

What might I need to quit?

When am I most likely to "should" all over myself and grudgingly accept requests?

How has pruning facilitated greater growth in my life?

3

But How Do I Say No?

We cannot do it all. We can't fulfill every request that people make of us. We cannot achieve every dream we have. We have to say no. But how on earth do we do it?

The first step to saying no is recognizing that we have a problem. We have to see that our lives are out of control because of so many yeses. We must admit that we're *yes-aholics*.

Perhaps that sounds a bit extreme. Our yes-aholism does not destroy our livers or impair our driving. Yes-aholism can even lead to professional *success*, at least early on. But it is rarely sustainable. Our yes-aholism can lead to burnout. We are far less likely to achieve what is most important when our attention is divided by what is good but not great. We have to say no.

In addition to recognizing that we have a problem, we also need to make a plan. Before we are even invited to take on another responsibility or pursue the next idea we have, we must prepare to say no. A military commander not only waits until the enemy attacks but also anticipates the other side's moves. He has strategies for dealing with various situations. He is proactive about building his defenses and warding off potential threats. We must take this same seriousness in preparing for the battle to say no.

Mindfulness of our weak points is critical. We can reflect on our various Achilles' heels—the people and situations that make it particularly difficult for us to say no. Like a squirrel saving nuts for winter, we need to prepare for the times when it will be more difficult for us to say no. What follows are some tools for assisting one's efforts.

Make a *Public* Commitment to Say No

There is a night-and-day difference between a commitment I make to myself and a commitment about which I tell others. If I make a personal commitment not to snack between meals, it is depressingly easy to renege on that commitment. I find myself opening the refrigerator when I'm hungry. Lord knows how many times I have told myself—and only myself—that I was going to do something, only to fail to do so. Sometimes, I last mere minutes.

If I tell friends and family members about my resolution, I am more likely to follow through with the commitment. If I say that I'm going to study a language or run a marathon, the people in my life will ask me about my training. Their interest pushes me to do what I told them I was going to do. If I tell my community members that I'm going to give up meat or alcohol for Lent, they will ask me why I'm eating a burger and drinking a beer. The very thought of seeing their questioning glances pushes me to do what I said I would do.

Looking back, I see times I wanted to do something but didn't *really* want to do something. I intentionally did not tell anyone else, knowing how powerful the pressure would be. And of course, I then did not follow through on the commitment that I pretended I wanted to make.

Making a public commitment changes the game. We act differently when we know that others can see whether we are making progress on our goals or fulfilling the commitments we made. Some people have found great success in losing weight by using Twitter. They share their diets and exercise routines. Some even weigh themselves and tweet their weight each week. This strategy is particularly effective for those who have a strong fear of social disapproval. Now, I have no interest in getting regular updates about someone's weight on Twitter. Then again, there is much on Twitter that I have no interest in. This at least sounds like a more productive use of the platform than most things on Twitter.

In fact, many people use the power of a public commitment to kick themselves off of social media addictions. LeBron James has often gone dark on social media during the NBA Playoffs to focus on basketball. Several of my friends fast from social media for Lent. If I saw them post or like, I would call them out on it. (I do not have the willpower to fast from social media myself, so I would see their activity.)

The marketing expert Seth Godin has been writing a daily blog for well over a decade. He never misses. This public commitment to consistency is a big part of his success. In discussing his regularity of writing, he notes, "Once a commitment is made to a streak the question shifts from, 'should I blog tomorrow,' to, 'what will tomorrow's blog say?' And once you've made that shift, it's 100x easier to find the voice that you're looking for."[29] Hundreds of thousands of people look forward to receiving his posts when we wake up in the morning. If Godin ever missed, he would hear from his fans.

Even if we do not have hundreds of thousands of followers, we probably know what Godin is talking about. Maybe our "public" is our workplace or church, but we know what it is like when people expect us to show up. Things would not be the same without our contribution, even if it's just a friendly face or warm greeting.

Make a Ulysses Pact That Locks You into a Future Decision

The spirit is willing, but the flesh is weak. It's an ancient problem that calls for an ancient solution. In the *Odyssey*, Ulysses (or Odysseus, in Greek) and his men must sail past the Sirens, whose enchanting songs cause passing sailors to crash. Ulysses's solution is to plug his men's ears with wax and have them bind him to the mast of his ship. His men will not hear the songs and thus continue sailing, while Ulysses can hear the Sirens without being doomed to death. Making a choice in the present that locks us into a particular decision in the future has become known as a Ulysses Pact or Ulysses Contract.

Even if someone does not know the term *Ulysses Pact*, we all do this—and we could benefit from doing it more often. I know someone who used a modern form of the Ulysses Pact to write a book. He went to a coffee shop each day with an old laptop stripped of everything but a word processor. He left his phone at home. After getting his coffee, he forced himself to sit down for a couple of hours. Of course, he would get bored. His mind would wander. He wanted to check his email or the scores of the game from the night before, but he couldn't. He could only write. *And he did.* He wrote that book faster than if he had allowed news feeds and phone notifications to distract him.

During the Spanish conquest of Mexico, the commander Hernán Cortés scuttled his own ships so that his men had no choice but to conquer or die. If we are going to accomplish what's most important and not get distracted by secondary projects, we may need to do something drastic. A Ulysses Contract could help lock us into saying no until we have finished what matters.

You have probably already engaged in various Ulysses Contracts. Perhaps you have a certain amount of your paycheck diverted to a retirement plan—removed from your checking account before you can spend it. Maybe you go to the grocery store after a meal rather than when your defenses are low because you're hungry. We can use these same techniques to pre-commit to saying no to the nonessential. We can then have time and energy for what matters.

Maybe you have a big project that you need to tackle, but your regular meetings and correspondence make it difficult. One strategy could be to block out an hour or two on your calendar every day. Treat it like you would treat a meeting with the pope or the president. If anyone asks to meet with you during your block, you could tell them, "Sorry, I have an appointment at that time." Turn your phone to airplane mode. If any calls or emails come in during that time, you could get back to them later and say, "Sorry, I had an appointment." A Ulysses Pact by which we lock ourselves into such "appointments" can give us the time and space to finally tackle big projects.

Replace "I Shouldn't" with "I *Don't*"

The very language we use can also help us say no. When trying not to say yes to too many things—or when trying to stop any unhelpful habit—say, "I don't," rather than "I shouldn't." Rather than say, "I shouldn't" take on more commitments, we can say, "I don't." *I don't* take on unnecessary tasks. *I don't* say yes to something without reflecting on what to cut. The change is subtle but powerful.

When I say I "shouldn't" eat that piece of cake or "shouldn't" waste time on social media, I use up willpower. I *might* resist social media or the cake this time, but after using up my energy to resist that temptation, I then indulge in some other bad habit. The same thing happens with commitments. When someone asks me to do something, I can spend all sorts of energy thinking about how I should learn to say no and create some boundaries. I might work up the power to decline the initial request and then find myself saying yes to the next five invitations.

Declining a request feels like a battle when using the language of "I shouldn't." The discomfort of hurting someone's feelings by saying no wears me down. "I don't" feels different. "I don't" is nonnegotiable. It's part of my identity. And every time I resist, I reaffirm this identity change rather than deplete my willpower.

Maybe we're not quite there yet. Maybe we haven't broken our bad habits. Maybe you're like me and still find yourself agreeing to too much. Still, say, "I don't." And then prove it to yourself with little victories. As prioritizing what's important becomes who you *are* rather than what you should do, the inability to say no has less of a grip on you.

The struggle to say no is an ongoing battle. In addition to the above tools, here are some questions to ask ourselves when we are considering a new commitment. We need all the help we can get.

Would I Say Yes to This If I Had to Do It Next Tuesday?

My calendar for next week looks awful. My calendar six months from now looks wide open. When someone asks me to do something next week, I often say no because I cannot even imagine how I would shoehorn in a new commitment. When someone asks me to do something months in advance, I can often think, *Sure, I have all the time in the world!* I often say yes—and then regret it later.

Most commitments would be simple if I had months to work on them. It's easy to agree to something when it's far off. But, of course, the intervening months will be filled with weeks that look like next week. Our day-to-day responsibilities do not stop. The little things that fill up our days—responding to e-mail, buying groceries, commuting to work—are not going away. The wide-open spaces currently in my calendar months from now are not going to be wide open for long.

The next time someone asks you to take on a new commitment, ask yourself, *Would I say yes to this if I had to do it next Tuesday?* We are aware of the many things we need to do between now and next Tuesday. This question gives us a realistic perspective on what it would look like to take on a new commitment.

Sometimes it makes sense to say yes. Sometimes we *have* to say yes. But not always. Some of the things we think we "should" do are unnecessary or better delegated to someone else. Some are good but function as obstacles to that which is great. Asking whether we would do something by next

Tuesday shows us the costs involved. We may need to cut back on sleep or recreation or time for other worthy projects. Asking the question slows us down and makes us recognize what we would be getting ourselves into.

Does This Make Me Say, "Hell Yeah!"?

Derek Sivers first gained prominence for founding CD Baby, an online distributor of independent music. Sivers has since received attention for his writing and speaking. He has some great advice for deciding whether to take on an opportunity that comes your way: "If you're not feeling 'Hell yeah, that would be awesome!' about something, say no." Sivers continues, "Refuse almost everything. Do almost nothing. But the things you do, do them all the way."[30]

Sivers identifies how many of us take on too many tepid commitments. We agree to do something, but our hearts are never really in it. We then become resentful. We say yes to too much and become worn down. Our many dispassionate commitments also tie us down and prevent us from seizing the next great opportunity.

Sivers is not the first to comment on these dynamics. Christ says something similar in the Gospel of Matthew: "Let your 'Yes' mean 'Yes,' and your 'No' mean 'No'" (Matthew

5:37). Perhaps we should translate that as "Let your 'Yes' mean 'Hell yes!' and your 'No' mean 'Hell no!'"

The hell-yeah-or-no question is only *a* tool—not the only tool. I'm not going to use a hammer and nails for everything that's broken. Sometimes duct tape works great. Similarly, asking, "Does this make me say, 'Hell yeah!'?" is helpful in many situations but not appropriate in others. There are many things that don't make us say, "Hell yeah!" but we do them to be decent and responsible human beings. Does a parent think, "Hell yeah, I get to change that diaper!" Probably not. But he should still change the diaper.

There are also periods in our lives when our hell-yeah-or-no filter needs to be stronger than at other times. If you have a career, young children, and responsibilities at church, you probably do not have time for many more commitments. Any new idea better make you say, "Hell yeah!" if you're going to squeeze it into your schedule. If you're a young musician or writer, however, you may need to say yes far more often. Writing for a tiny magazine or performing at a random bar on a Monday night may not make you say, "Hell yeah!" Still, such experiences could help you get your reps in to develop your craft and establish a name for yourself. Those mediocre commitments could pave the way for many "hell yeah!" moments down the line.

Another way of using the "hell yeah!" test is to imagine yourself accepting the request that you are considering and then later hearing that it has been canceled. For example, let's say you agree to serve on a committee for a community organization. Meetings are scheduled. You block out time in your calendar. And then the day before the first meeting, you hear that the committee is no longer going to gather. If your reaction to the news is a hearty "hell yeah!", that's a strong sign that this is not actually something that you want to do. Now, you may not have much of a choice in the matter, but if you do have a choice, the "hell yeah!" test can illuminate what you feel, not what you think you should feel.

What Would I Tell My Best Friend to Do in This Situation?

The next time you're stuck and unable to decide whether to take on a new commitment, ask yourself, "What would I tell my best friend in this situation?" You might find that things become clear.

When we are the ones in the middle of a decision, there's baggage. We're emotionally invested. We can be afraid of disappointing others. We don't want to rock the boat by saying no. We don't want people to see us as lazy or ungrateful or incapable. We might focus on the worst possible thing that could happen. We often can't see the forest for the trees.

When we're advising our best friend, however, we're detached from short-term emotions. We can recognize the signs of overcommitment and the need to say no. We can separate the wheat from the chaff and see the big picture. Advising a friend can even become a game to figure out the best possible path forward. We want our friend to do what's best. The decision that a friend is struggling with might appear obvious to us.

So, when deciding, shift your perspective and imagine you are advising your best friend. Give your "friend" advice—and then follow it for yourself. You might find that the fog of uncertainty lifts. We can know what *we* should do because we know what *they* should do.

What Would Be the Most Courageous Thing to Do?

When I was in college, I was a nerd. Well, let's be honest, I still am a nerd. Anyway, one year for Halloween, two friends and I dressed as the three Brothers Karamazov because of our shared love for Dostoevsky's classic novel. I went as Alyosha, the monk, and wore a cassock to the party. By dressing up as a religious person, I found myself wanting to act like a religious person. I was more mindful of how much I drank at that Halloween party than I normally would have been.

Sometimes we know that we should say no to the requests that come our way, but we struggle to do so. We're afraid of hurting someone's feelings by declining the invitation. In that case, we can ask ourselves, *What would the most courageous version of myself do?* By trying to act like the courageous versions of ourselves, we become more courageous. It's kind of like spiritual fake-it-till-you-make-it.

What Will Enlarge My Life?

We've surely heard people tell us, "Do what makes you happy." It sounds so simple. As long as something isn't immoral or illegal, why *wouldn't* we do what makes us happy?

In practice, it's not so easy. We might *think* that a particular path in life is going to make us happy, but it doesn't always turn out that way. Our initial excitement may fade. Additionally, our lives are bound up with other people. How do we navigate our own happiness with that of our families, friends, and those most in need?

The truth is, we often don't know what's going to make us happy. It's better to pursue what is meaningful. Rather than ask, "Will this make me happy?" we could ask, "Will this enlarge or diminish my life?" Sometimes, that will mean putting aside our superficial desires and doing something good for another person. At other times, it will mean saying no to a request or stepping away from a commitment that is getting in the way of our most important relationships. If we choose enlargement, we might find that happiness—ours and others'—comes along as a great side effect.

Saying no is *not* about deprivation. We can use these tools and questions to help us say no *in order to give a deeper yes*. We say no so that we can say (hell) yes to what matters. It's hard to find meaning when we are being stretched in so many different directions. Less is more. We say no to say yes to a more abundant life.

What Can I Do Now?

I learned how to worry more about how I felt and less about "what people might think." I was setting new boundaries and began to let go of my need to please, perform, and perfect. I started saying no rather than sure (and being resentful and pissed off later). I began to say "Oh, hell yes!" rather than "Sounds fun, but I have lots of work to do."[31]

—Brené Brown

What are my weak points when it comes to saying no? What are the types of situations in which I am most likely to say yes and regret it later?

Have I ever had extra stick-to-itiveness by making a commitment public? If so, what happened?

What Ulysses Pact might I make to pre-commit to something I want to achieve?

What current or potential commitments make me want to say, "Hell yeah!"?

ACCEPTING NO

4

Turn It into Compost

It's important to learn to say no, but we often don't have any say in the matter. Instead, *life* tells us no. You don't get the job. A relationship fizzles. An accident occurs. A global pandemic forces you to rearrange your plans—and it doesn't even have the decency to ask how you feel about it all!

This should not surprise us. It's part of the human experience. If I asked you whether you expected to get everything that you wanted without any problems, I hope you would laugh in my face. Of course it's not going to be smooth sailing. We learn from an early age that life isn't fair. And yet when we experience problems—even though *we know life isn't fair*—we can find ourselves asking, "Why is this happening to me?"

Perhaps that response is not surprising. Our lives are far more comfortable and predictable than our ancestors could have dreamed of. We can delude ourselves into thinking that we have more control than we do. But then life punches us in the face. Despite extensive planning, there are some things we cannot expect or control.

Some responses to the trials of life are more helpful than others. One possible response is denial. We could pretend that everything is fine, that there's *nothing to see here*! Such a response will not end well. We may want to deny difficult realities, but denial doesn't change the disappointment or death or destruction.

Another response is to acknowledge the bad that has taken place and then go through life with a chip on our shoulder. This is often evident in our behavior. We snap. We lose our patience. We wear our anger on our faces. Pope Francis has said that some Christians' lives "seem like Lent without Easter."[32] They conduct themselves "like someone who has just come back from a funeral!"[33]

Legend has it that Abraham Lincoln was once advised to include someone on his cabinet. The person had all the qualifications for the job, but Lincoln told his advisers that he didn't like the man's face. Exasperated, they told him that he couldn't exclude him because of his looks, for which he was not responsible. Lincoln retorted, "Every man over forty is responsible for his face."[34] If we are resentful, people will notice. It will show up on our faces. Lincoln did not want a bitter man on his cabinet.

Sometimes life gives us a bitter pill to swallow, but sometimes we swallow more of those bitter pills than we need to.

We allow resentment to eat away at us. We have all known a person whose negativity threatens to bring down everyone around them. We have likely been that person at one time or another. Such negativity is toxic.

Those who are angriest aren't necessarily those who have suffered the most. There's often little correlation. After a certain number of years, we have all experienced enough heartache and disappointment to be bitter. But not everyone goes there. Some people do not get pulled down. They're durable. They continue as if nothing has happened to them.

But many people respond in an even better manner. They are not just durable; they are antifragile. They experience post-traumatic *growth*. They turn their disappointment into the fuel for greatness.

Frustration as Fuel

"Someone should do something!" We've probably all said it. And maybe that "someone" is you. Or me.

Jordan Peterson describes the following "rule" in his book *Beyond Order*: "Notice that opportunity lurks where responsibility has been abdicated."[35]

Peterson notes that we can get frustrated with the government, our boss, and all sorts of other people who are not taking responsibility. We can feel outraged that what needs to be done is not being done.

But that outrage can be a doorway—an invitation to us to make a contribution. Perhaps it's small. Our sphere of influence may be limited. But trying to do our part is going to be far more meaningful than complaining about what someone else is not doing. Plus, if we're contributing rather than complaining, it's going to be far more pleasant for other people to have us around!

Our frustration can be revealing. When we experience righteous anger, that might be a space where we need to do some good.

The Refiner's Fire

What do George Washington, Abraham Lincoln, Gandhi, the Brontë sisters, Michelangelo, Dante, and Bach have in common? They each lost a parent during childhood.

Malcolm Gladwell dedicated a chapter of his book *David and Goliath* to "eminent orphans."[36] Gladwell cites the work of a psychologist, Marvin Eisenstadt, who found people whose biographies were more than one column long in an encyclopedia. This was a rough approximation of a person's eminence. Of those who met this threshold, more than a third had lost a parent by the age of fifteen. Those who had a parent die during childhood were disproportionately likely to become eminent.

I know from experience that losing a parent during childhood is tragic. I would never wish that on anyone, even if some study indicates that orphans are more likely to become president or prime minister. Those who lose a parent early in life are also more likely to end up in prison. The death of a mother or father can be crushing.

But not always. A child who has lost a parent knows that bad things happen. Through such tragedy, some develop resilience to conquer future challenges. They have gone through the refiner's fire. They are more likely to reach the pinnacles of success than those who have not been tested in such a way. We would never wish such a tragedy on a child, and yet our societies often depend on those who have been tested in this manner.

Surprisingly Resilient

We don't really know how negative experiences will affect us. We may assume the worst, but our assumptions can be wrong.

In the years leading up to World War II, British military planners worried about a German bombing of London. They knew they were vulnerable to an air assault. They assumed that this would be devastating for the British people. One military planner said, "London for several days will be one vast raving bedlam. The hospitals will be stormed, traffic will cease, the homeless will shriek for help, the city will be a pandemonium."[37]

The Germans did bomb London. They caused significant destruction. People died. But there was no pandemonium. Instead, morale soared. Social solidarity increased. The British people were far more resilient than the planners expected. With their characteristic stiff upper lip, the British *increased* their war production during the months of the bombings.

Such an experience is not an anomaly. Our "psychological immune system" is often stronger than we expect. One can find many examples of how a crisis brings people together and produces some positive outcomes. In the months following the attacks of September 11, 2001, there was a dramatic *decrease* in suicide in New York City and surrounding areas.[38] Tragedies have a way of shaking us out of our navel gazing and pushing us to see the bigger picture. We often grow closer to others.

Art Supplies

The Argentinian writer Jorge Luis Borges said, "A writer—and, I believe, generally all persons—must think that whatever happens to him or her is a resource. . . . All that happens to us, including our humiliations, our misfortunes, our embarrassments, all is given to us as raw material, as clay, so that we may shape our art."[39]

This is true not only for writers. Think of a comedian. Some of the best comics make fun of themselves. They use their struggles and embarrassing moments as material to get the crowd to laugh—and invite listeners to laugh at their own imperfections.

John D. Rockefeller Sr. said, "Oh, how blessed young men are who have to struggle for a foundation and beginning in life." *Blessed* are those who have to struggle? It sounds so cruel. Who wants to see a young person struggle? That goes against every instinct of a parent or teacher. But Rockefeller knew this from experience. His learning from early challenges helped him later become the richest man in America.

Aleksandr Solzhenitsyn was no stranger to intense suffering. The Russian writer was accused of anti-Soviet propaganda and sentenced to eight years in a labor camp. Still, he writes in *The Gulag Archipelago*, "I turn back to the years of my imprisonment and say, sometimes to the astonishment of those about me: 'Bless you, prison! . . . Bless you, prison, for having been my life.'"[40]

Bless you, *prison*? And not just any prison, but bless you, *Soviet labor camp*? Solzhenitsyn's experience of prison was that of the refiner's fire. He learned about the human condition. And he shared that with the world. Some have called his *Gulag Archipelago* the most important book of the twentieth century.

Burden University

Our burdens can be our greatest teachers. Benjamin Franklin said that the things that hurt are the things that instruct. Some of the best priests for confession are those who have wrestled with addiction. It's material out of which they can minister.

As much as we can lament our difficulties, if there are no problems, there's no progress. Our difficulties might tempt us to curl up into a ball. But we can also use them to bulk up and get stronger. Pope Francis writes in *Fratelli Tutti*, "Difficulties that seem overwhelming are opportunities for growth, not excuses for a glum resignation that can lead only to acquiescence."[41]

We also need to grieve. I'm not going to tell someone who is mourning, "Wow, you could write a great book about this!" I'm not going to tell someone who has just lost her business, "But think of the life lessons you have learned!" We need time to process our difficulties. Someone else cannot demand that we "get over it," and we cannot demand that of others.

But grief does not need to be the end of the story. Life has offered us all a lot of material—and life is not finished! We could see our failures and misfortunes as a burden, but we could also see them as a resource—for art, for understanding, for connection.

Leonard Cohen sang that there is a crack in everything; that's how the light gets in.[42] Sometimes there are *many* cracks. We are blinded by the light. It can be a bit much. We wish that we didn't have to go through so many grades in the school of life, so many "opportunities for growth." We could—and often do—complain. But we could also use it as a resource.

The Gift of Jerks

Jerks are a gift. At least they can be. The best way of getting back at a jerk is to turn him into your teacher. Just as we can destroy our enemies by making them our friends, we can remove the jerks from our lives by making them our instructors. We can see what we *don't* want to become. It's important to have role models. It's also important to have antimodels—those people who make us say, "Wow, I never want to be like *that* guy!"

Perhaps an ex hurt you. That same person may have taught you about healthy boundaries. We may see how we need to grow in patience. Perhaps we notice that we do the exact same thing and hurt others. Edmund Burke said, "He that wrestles with us strengthens our nerves and sharpens our skill. Our antagonist is our helper."[43]

Socrates had a wife who was hard to get along with. Granted, we have only his side of the story. I wonder what she said about him. One time she was so angry with Socrates that she poured the contents of a chamber pot on his head. His response: "After thunder comes the rain."[44] As difficult as his marriage was, it was great for his work of philosophy. He better understood the human condition.

We can learn a lot from people who are difficult to get along with. (Others might find *us* hard to get along with! A jerk is in the eye of the beholder.) One strategy is to make it a game. One faces more-challenging enemies as one reaches higher levels in a video game. We can treat every jerk we meet as another opponent who can then push us to the next level.

Reasons for Desolation

In his "Rules for Discernment" from *The Spiritual Exercises*, St. Ignatius describes consolation and desolation. Consolation is every increase in faith, hope, and love. It's accompanied by experiences such as peace, joy, and courage. Desolation is the reverse. It's every decrease in faith, hope, and love. Characteristic experiences in desolation include apathy, agitation, and fear.

God does not *send* us desolation. God does not play around with us just to see how we will respond. Still, God *permits* desolation. One can ask why. Why would God permit this unpleasant experience? Isn't God supposed to be love?

In *The Spiritual Exercises*, Ignatius proposes three reasons for desolation. First, sometimes desolation is our fault. We fail to pray. We're lazy when it comes to the spiritual life. Desolation can remind us to get our spiritual house in order. But sometimes desolation is not our fault. Even the holiest people in the world experience it. Why would this be?

The second reason that Ignatius gives for desolation is that it can test how far we will push ourselves in the service and praise of God. We can learn a lot about ourselves and God through desolation—lessons we would not learn if we were in constant consolation.

Spending time in prayer is a pleasure when it's joyful and inspiring. But what about the (many) times when it's dry or boring or lifeless? What about serving God when it's unpopular? When we get rejected? Desolation can push us to see whether we want to be with *God* or whether we want a *God high*.

Last, desolation can cultivate humility. We see that we can't do things alone. We have a role to play, but we are always dependent on God. That becomes clear when experiencing desolation. We would not grow as much in the spiritual life without passing through periods of dryness, just as people who live through winter are more appreciative of beautiful, warm weather.

"Weather" or Not

When I was in college, I studied for a semester in Kampala, Uganda. Kampala is near the equator but at an elevation of about four thousand feet. This leads to perfect weather conditions. They have a low of sixty-five degrees and a high of eighty pretty much every day of the year. I'm not *not* jealous.

While the people of Kampala are resilient in so many areas of their lives, their tolerance for temperature variations is a different story. They can't stand it if the weather happens to go outside that fifteen-degree window. If it's eighty-four, people will complain about how hot it is. If it gets down to sixty-two, people will grab a blanket and complain about how cold it is. I can't help but think, *You don't know what cold is!*

Even for those of us who live in places that see greater temperature extremes, we have it relatively easy. Few (sane) people like months of snow and ice, but most of us have a warm home and workplace to go to. A summer of heat and humidity is unpleasant, but many of us move from an air-conditioned building to an air-conditioned car to another air-conditioned building.

It's comfortable to be able to control the temperature, but that doesn't mean pleasant temperatures are always good for us. Many people in recent years have talked about the health benefits of cold showers. One of my idiosyncrasies is walking to and from work, even during the heart of winter. I am convinced that I'm less likely to get sick because I get lots of fresh air. Granted, stubbornness, not science, shapes my view. Please check with your doctor!

There do seem to be some psychological benefits to starting one's day by choosing to take a cold shower or trudge through the snow. It's a small win. It's a way to say, *Hey, I'm not a total weakling.* No matter what happens the rest of the day, this day will not be a failure because I have already earned a victory. Choosing to become a little uncomfortable prevents us from seeing every molehill of annoyance as a mountain of frustration.

New Growth Is Possible

There are few simple pleasures as fascinating to me as compost. Throw a bunch of stuff that is seemingly good for nothing—banana peels, leaves, coffee grounds, fruit rinds, grass clippings—into a pile. Make sure there's some moisture. Toss it around from time to time so that it gets some oxygen to allow bacteria to have a party. And then watch in amazement as it all breaks down into a happy black substance that is perfect for a garden.

We normally send the same materials to a landfill, where they take up space and give off methane—a greenhouse gas far worse than carbon dioxide. But these exact same "waste" materials can create compost and nourish a garden. Much of what one needs to grow something beautiful might be in the wastebasket. It's like multiplying a negative by a negative and getting a positive.

These principles aren't limited to our gardens. We can also allow the deaths and disappointments we have experienced to nourish new life.

We could focus on all we are missing out on, all the hurts we have experienced. Or we could allow our negative experiences to produce new life—to make us more resilient, more compassionate, more grateful for all that we have. It's not about denying the pain or pretending that the disappointment is imaginary. But pain and disappointment do not have to be the end of the story.

The COVID-19 crisis rocked the world in countless ways. It was heartbreaking to see the loss of life and the closure of businesses. But we also saw much good come out of the tragedy. People stepped forward to care for the vulnerable. Companies innovated in delivering goods and services. Researchers made advances in medical technology. We can hope that we're better prepared to tackle future pandemics.

As novel as the coronavirus and lockdown were to many of us, a pandemic is nothing new in human history—nor is the use of such situations for some good. Isaac Newton made major advances in the development of calculus when he was in lockdown due to the plague. Shakespeare may have written *King Lear* when in quarantine.

It doesn't mean that we skip over the loss of life, the pain of unemployment, or the sadness in not being able to gather. Those things are true, but they are not the whole story. Our greatest tragedies can become our greatest opportunities for growth. People as diverse as Friedrich Nietzsche and Kelly Clarkson—how's that for a pair!—have talked about how what doesn't kill us makes us stronger.

Of course, it's not always the case. Some people break. Some people go through trauma and are never the same. Post-traumatic stress is real.

But so is post-traumatic growth. The single biggest factor in growing from failure or tragedy is the belief that new life is possible. The worst things that have happened to us do not have to define us. The learning expert Jim Kwik often says, "If you fight for your limitations, you get to keep them."[45] Those limitations are an option, not an inevitability.

Whenever life tells us no, we can lament what we've lost, or we can treat this time like compost and allow it to produce new life. When we're in the middle of disappointment, it might look like a whole lot of manure. But this exact same experience might be what can feed our future growth.

What Can I Do Now?

Above all, trust in the slow work of God. We are quite naturally impatient in everything to reach the end without delay. We should like to skip the intermediate stages. We are impatient of being on the way to something unknown, something new. And yet it is the law of all progress that it is made by passing through some stages of instability—and that it may take a very long time.

And so, I think it is with you; your ideas mature gradually—let them grow, let them shape themselves, without undue haste. Don't try to force them on, as though you could be today what time (that is to say, grace and circumstances acting on your own good will) will make of you tomorrow. Only God could say what this new spirit gradually forming within you will be. Give Our Lord the benefit of believing that his hand is leading you, and accept the anxiety of feeling yourself in suspense and incomplete.[46]

When has life shown me that *I'm not in control*?

Have I ever experienced post-traumatic *growth*? If so, what happened? How have the various cracks in my life allowed the light to come in?

"If you fight for your limitations, you get to keep them." Where do I see this in my own life?

How have I been "blessed" by my struggles?

5

Freed by Constraints

Some of the most creative poetry in recent decades has been about *canned meat*. Thousands of people have taken up the challenge to write a haiku about *SPAM*. Yes, SPAM. John Nagamichi Cho describes himself as a "meat poet," as opposed to a Beat poet.[47] He set up the SPAM Haiku Archive in 1995. Thousands of compositions about the canned meat came pouring in from people all over the world.

The results have been hilarious. You can go down a rabbit hole of SPAM haiku on the Internet. Here are two of my favorites: "Pink beefy temptress / I can no longer remain / Vegetarian." "I sometimes wonder / If what Dahmer left in fridge / Was shipped to Hormel."[48]

The three-line haiku has significant constraints. Its lines must have five syllables, seven syllables, and five syllables. That's it. And then you take that limited form and apply it to *SPAM*? The exercise is preposterously constrained.

And that's exactly why it works. The flourishing of creative poetry is not in spite of the limitations; it's because of them.

Constraints foster creativity. If I said to you, "Tell me something funny," you might struggle to respond. If I said, "Tell me a knock-knock joke," you could think of one immediately. The rigid formula of a haiku and the ridiculous subject matter of SPAM provide helpful scaffolding for creativity.

Need more evidence? Theodor Geisel once made a bet with his editor that he could write an entire book using only fifty unique words. It sounds impossible. A book with a vocabulary limited to fifty different words? Well, Geisel won the bet—and a lot more than that from earnings on the book. You may better know Geisel as Dr. Seuss. And that book? Perhaps you've heard of it. It's called *Green Eggs and Ham*. Rather than being an obstacle, the significant restrictions pushed Geisel to be more creative. Generations of children have benefited.

Obstacles Are Opportunities

Insufficient freedom is a bad thing, but that doesn't mean that a life without limits is a good thing. *Total freedom is false freedom*. An unconstrained life does not work. We need boundaries. We find freedom through constraints.

Encountering those constraints is not always pleasant. We often lament the obstacles in our way. We can focus on what we are missing. We yearn for more time or a bigger budget. We wish we had other people's natural talents. We mourn the loss of loved ones. We get rejected. We struggle to accept the many times that life constrains our plans.

But the obstacle in our path may be the avenue by which we can grow and get better. Necessity really is the mother of invention. We may not know how we're going to get through a particular challenge, but we also know that we have faced uncertainty before. And we have become stronger by overcoming previous obstacles. We could complain about the roadblocks. Or we could allow them to show us a new and better path.

The Beauty of the Game

Any sport has rules. Disregarding the rules to be "free" does not result in free play. Rather, you would have anarchy or boredom. If there were no limitations on how and when a defensive end could hit a quarterback, things would soon get ugly. If there were no penalties for going out of bounds in a sport, then there would be no effort to stay within the lines (and no heated arguments about whether the player's foot was in). Fans would soon lose interest.

Now, all sorts of strange rules have accrued over the years in various sports. Why is the shot clock in the NBA twenty-four seconds rather than twenty-five? I don't know. It just is. But it's a better experience when everyone agrees to the same seemingly arbitrary number. Playing within the rules of a sport, rather than trying to change them as you go along, can lead to the beauty of the game.

In 2017, I started the "One-Minute Homily," a series of video reflections on social media for *The Jesuit Post*. Saying something of substance in a short amount of time takes a lot of work. Someone once said, "If you want me to speak for an hour, I am ready today. If you want me to speak for just a few minutes, it will take me a few weeks to prepare." Similarly, I can stand up anywhere and start talking. That's not a problem (well, except for the people who have to listen to me gab). What takes work is figuring out what is worth saying and what I need to cut. And when I have only a minute, I have to cut not only the crazy stuff and the boring stuff. I also must cut the decent-but-not-great stuff. It is painful.

But it forces me to get better. The time limit pushes me to get to the point. I don't always strike the right balance between brevity and substance. Still, I'm more likely to convey a message in a format that people with a limited attention span (like myself) might watch until the end.

Knocked Down but Not Out

The Great Chicago Fire of 1871 was devastating. About 300 people died. Roughly a third of the residents of the city were left homeless. Still, the pressure to rebuild and the blank slate with which to work led to an architectural revolution. Skyscrapers rose from the ashes, transforming Chicago and influencing cities around the world. Chicago soon became far more populous and prosperous than before.

A similar story has happened with other places forced to deal with limitations. Manhattan is an island. There is only so much space—on land. But buildings were able to extend higher and higher into the sky. Israel has a limited supply of fresh water. In response, Israel has become a world leader in desalination and water-saving technology. Singapore is an island city-state with one of the highest population densities in the world. It has become an innovator in reclaiming land from the sea. Constraints foster creativity.

Conversely, experts discuss the "resource curse" or "paradox of plenty." Violent conflict, lagging economies, and low levels of democracy have plagued many resource-rich countries. There are plenty of exceptions to this. Oil-rich countries such as Canada and Norway are doing just fine. Still, an abundance of resources can lead to an abundance of problems. Corruption festers. There's less pressure to produce an educated workforce. Not enough attention is given to efficiency. Violence is all too common.

One does not need to go to another country to see this dynamic. Growing up rich can create its own sort of "resource curse." A person may never develop a great work ethic because he never *has* to if things are always provided for him.

Many people who grow up privileged turn out to be wonderful human beings. Additionally, money covers many problems; it's a lot harder to fall through the cracks if you have a safety net. Still, many successful people experienced considerable constraints while growing up. A significant number of new millionaires are first- or second-generation immigrants. A disproportionate number of CEOs suffer from dyslexia. Many of those most skilled in the helping professions have had to deal with trauma. Privilege can come with its own share of obstacles to flourishing, while having to overcome hardships can lead to later success.

Constrain to Grow

If we are stagnant in some areas of our lives, we may need to impose some constraints. When I have all the time in the world, I easily become complacent. If I have a hard deadline, I become a machine. I can get more done in a day than I normally accomplish in a week. And if I don't have a deadline? I'm much better off making up a deadline and sticking to it.

Constraints are particularly important in raising children. Unless parents put limits on what their kids may and may not eat, their kids' diets may consist of little more than Goldfish crackers and chicken nuggets. We stunt the growth of young people if we provide everything they desire. While we ought to do what we can to provide an environment of reasonable physical safety, even that has limits. Do we get rid of stoves to prevent a child from burning his hand? Do we scrap recess so that a kid never falls down and skins his knee? I'm glad that I did not grow up in such an environment, even though I have the scars to prove it.

There are many indications that we have not gotten the balance right in recent years. Jonathan Haidt and Greg Lukianoff make a convincing case that "safetyism" has contributed to skyrocketing rates of anxiety and depression among young people. Their book *The Coddling of the American Mind* argues that parents' good intentions may set their kids up for failure.[49] "Bulldozer parents" who remove all obstacles in their children's path can prevent their kids from developing resiliency to deal with life's challenges.

With a father who is a United States Senator, Ben Sasse's children would not need to get a job to put food on the table. Still, Sasse believes he learned about hard work growing up by detasseling corn and walking beans in Nebraska.[50] He wants his children to learn similar lessons. Thus, he sent his fourteen-year-old daughter to work on a cattle ranch and help deliver hundreds of calves. Sasse believes that kids need to suffer a bit. Removing obstacles from their path stunts their growth. Helping them develop an appreciation for hard work is one of the greatest gifts a parent can give a child.

Controlling Ourselves before Getting Controlled

Just because we *could* do something does not mean that we *should* do something. Most of us have more food, drink, and entertainment available to us than our ancestors could have dreamed of. That does not mean we should always give in to our passing desires. We need practices that help us keep things under control rather than let the things we consume control us.

People of different religious traditions see value in practices that constrain us. Jews refrain from work on the Sabbath. Catholics give up something for Lent. Muslims fast from sunrise to sunset throughout the month of Ramadan (and make a Catholic fast look like a piece of cake). Some people take a "digital sabbath" one day a week as they navigate their relationships with their various electronic devices. Edmund Burke wrote, "Men of intemperate minds cannot be free. Their passions forge their fetters."[51] Such practices help tame the passions. We realize that we can skip a meal or refrain from work one day per week and be just fine—or more than fine. We often feel better after disconnecting from our devices or consuming less. These constraints free us.

Such imposed constraints also prepare us for future constraints that are out of our hands. Most of us could benefit from making some things harder than they have to be. We might bike to work, even if we could get there faster in a car. We could have a difficult-but-needed conversation with someone rather than ignore a problem. As a result, we become less afraid of addressing thorny issues in the future. We toughen up in the process—and prepare for the times when things are harder than we want them to be. If I'm addicted to pleasant situations, then I will be less willing to take a risk. I'll stay with the status quo and miss out on what could be great. Imposing some constraints can enable us to feel free in any situation.

Less Is More

"All work and no play makes Jack a dull boy." The truth is, all work doesn't even make Jack a productive boy! Jack is more likely to experience burnout and make mistakes because he is fatigued and unable to think clearly. We're unlikely to succeed without working hard. But that doesn't mean that more work is always the answer. There is more to life than success.

And doing less can even enable us to do more. After a certain point, there is no correlation between time worked and creative output. We are men and women, not machines. Productivity drops significantly beyond fifty hours of work in a week. One study found that those who worked seventy hours in a week were no more productive than those who worked fifty-five hours.[52] If we're running around like headless chickens or falling asleep at our desks, we're unlikely to have creative breakthroughs. The philosopher Søren Kierkegaard said, "I have walked myself into my best thoughts."[53]

You may have heard of the "10,000-hour rule," popularized by Malcolm Gladwell in his book *Outliers*.[54] "10,000 Hours" even became the title of a Justin Bieber song! The idea is that world-class performance comes after 10,000 hours of deliberate practice. Still, the original study Gladwell used to develop the idea also showed that elite performers *slept* much more than average performers. Many were avid nappers.

High achievers are also more likely to engage in hobbies. They're intentional both in their work and in their recreation. Alex Soojung-Kim Pang, author of *Rest: Why You Get More Done When You Work Less*, argues that many of the most creative and productive people in history weren't accomplished despite their leisure; they were accomplished because of it.[55]

If we want to succeed, we need a lot of deliberate practice, but we also need deliberate rest.

Fast in Order to Feast

Accepting our constraints and imposing additional limitations is not just about doing more; it's also about *being* more. Constraints lead to deeper enjoyment. If I drink only amazing beer, it stops tasting amazing. My enjoyment of a craft IPA is greater when I also drink the cheap stuff and have a point of comparison. If I use air conditioning every day in the summer, I take the AC for granted. If I regularly use a fan, then the occasional air conditioning feels *amazing*. A mountaintop view is far more satisfying if you climb the mountain rather than drive up it. You might have some sore legs, but you're going to have more satisfaction.

I am not advocating puritanism. We simply enjoy a feast more when we have experienced some fasting. We're often better off with a simple option, even if we could afford something else. If we choose what's most comfortable or pleasurable all the time, then nothing feels like a treat. When wonderful experiences are rare, then they really are wonderful. Simplicity can lead to abundance.

During my senior year of college, I lived in a neighborhood where break-ins were quite common. My housemates and I had a masterful security system. It involved not having anything of value. It worked great! No one wanted to take our thrift-store furniture, and there was a total absence of electronics.

The novelists Kurt Vonnegut and Joseph Heller were once at a party given by a billionaire. Vonnegut asked Heller, "How does it make you feel that our host only yesterday may have made more money than your novel *Catch-22* has earned in its entire history?"

"I've got something he can never have," Heller responded. "The knowledge that I've got enough."[56]

I don't mean to play down the reality of people around the world who do not have enough. But many of us—certainly anyone with the money and time to buy and read this book—have more than enough. We have storage units full of stuff. We try to get rid of everything that does not "spark joy" because we're imprisoned by our stuff. But then we go and accumulate more. We buy things for convenience, but then our mountains of possessions become inconvenient to deal with. Our stuff traps us.

St. Josemaría Escrivá said, "He has most who needs least." With less stuff, there's less we have to think about. Simplicity is not about deprivation; it's about abundance. Constraints foster freedom.

The Freedom of Institutions

Joining institutions is a significant way we constrain ourselves, but these days we are joining fewer groups. As Robert Putnam documented in· *Bowling Alone*, there has been a significant decline in institutions such as bowling leagues and fraternal organizations.[57] Church participation has been going down for decades. Involvement in parent-teacher organizations is well below its peak. Fewer workers are members of private-sector labor unions. People today have fewer institutional commitments.

Such groups are becoming less popular but no less needed. Ditching institutions might appear to be freeing, but it's actually isolating. We miss out on friendship and love and loyalty. We miss out on webs of connections that make us better human beings. When people expect us to contribute to a shared enterprise, we are far more likely to turn off Netflix and do something productive. If I see someone at church every weekend, then I'm able to recognize his or her humanity. We might disagree on politics but agree on what is more important. If, instead, I sit in my social media silo, I can think the worst of people who aren't in my "tribe." Institutional commitments shake us out of our navel gazing.

The institution that shows these dynamics most clearly is the family. Family life is all about constraints. Responsible parents set limits for their children. As kids, we resented the constraints imposed on us. As adults, we thank God that our parents set such limits. We have all seen spoiled children; it's not a pretty sight. Growing up, I would have been delighted to eat nothing but Lucky Charms. I count my lucky stars that this had no chance of flying in our house. I may not have liked the limits at the time, but I'm grateful now for how they set me free.

While children feel that their parents impose the constraints, children set greater limitations on the freedom of their parents. When new parents hold their child in their arms for the first time, many think, *$**t just got real!* And interrupted sleep gets real. Worries about the health and safety of their children get real. Limitations on traveling and getting together with friends get real. The question "Should I really be doing this?" gets real for a mother or father.

Such responsibilities constrain us but also empower us. They stretch us and break open our hearts. They make us grow up. We see that this is not a game. People count on us, and we don't want to let them down. We develop as human persons through the constraints that come with responsibilities.

In *Evangelii Gaudium*, Pope Francis writes about how sometimes Christians "are tempted to keep the Lord's wounds at arm's length." Still, the pope writes, Christ wants his followers to "stop looking for those personal or communal niches which shelter us from the maelstrom of human misfortune and instead enter into the reality of other people's lives and know the power of tenderness." Francis continues, "Whenever we do so, our lives become wonderfully complicated."[58]

What a perfect phrase—*wonderfully complicated*. Taking on responsibility and entering the messiness of people's lives will bring complications. But it is a higher form of living. It is wonderful to be part of a cause bigger than ourselves.

It's not easy to run up against our constraints. We miss the free time we used to have. We can lament the heavy load of responsibility. When we run into obstacles, we often don't see them as learning opportunities. Instead, we might see them as roadblocks. We complain.

We can focus on all that we are missing out on. But if we scratch a little deeper, we can also see what we gain. The things that seem to constrain us are the very things that free us.

What Can I Do Now?

What I didn't understand—couldn't have, at the time—was that deserting yourself for another person really is a relief. My days began to unfold according to her schedule, that weird rhythm of newborns, and the worries I entertained were better than the ones that came before: more concrete, more vital, less tethered to the claustrophobic confines of my own skull. For this member of a generation famously beset by anxiety, it was a welcome liberation.[59]

—Elizabeth Bruenig

How have my problems fostered my progress? How has a weakness pushed me to develop some strength?

When have I opted for less and received more in return?

What helps me feel that I have "enough"?

How have my responsibilities led me to become a better human being?

6

Good-Enough Greatness

You meet the woman or man of your dreams—or so you think—but then you discover something that isn't so great about the person. You hope to make a contribution at work but see that there are people who are much more talented. You intend to tackle some big creative project, but you don't have nearly as much time as you expected.

You could give up. You could break up with the person and wait for the perfect mate. You could do the minimum at work, knowing that even if you gave your maximum, other people would be better. You could ditch your plans and give up on the creative project. Without enough time, it would never turn out the way you would like.

But you could also move forward, despite the less-than-ideal circumstances. That person may not be perfect, but then again, who is? They might still make a wonderful life partner. You may rarely be the most talented person in the workplace, but you can still contribute. You may not have the time you would like, but when do you ever have the time you would like? You can still create with the time that you have.

Things don't turn out the way we hope. Life happens. And life is not always kind. Some of our plans may no longer be possible. But other paths forward remain. We may not have the time or resources we expected. But we surely have *some* time and resources. It was never going to be perfect. We can accept it. And get to work.

If I keep plugging away with a mindset of "it's good enough," things might actually turn out great. If I wait around for perfect conditions before moving forward, I will often be waiting for a very long time. A less-than-perfect something is far better than nonexistent perfection.

Running Away from Imperfection

I had to leave. Things had been great for my first semester with the Jesuits, but I then became convinced that I had to leave. While I had met many inspiring Jesuits, I had also seen some of the warts of the Society of Jesus that were not clear to me before I entered. While I knew many excellent priests, I also saw how destructive clericalism could be. I wanted nothing to do with it. I didn't want to cast my lot with an imperfect institution.

This thinking took place during a thirty-day silent retreat. I figured it would be silly to leave in the middle of the experience. I would finish the retreat and then say goodbye to my plans to become a Jesuit priest.

In the meantime, I kept praying. I spent time picturing Jesus Christ in the various Gospel scenes. Christians believe that the omnipotent, omniscient God became one of *us*. The second person of the Trinity became like us in all ways but sin. And it's not as if this God-become-man lived apart from us. He worked a normal job. His followers were not products of elite institutions. Christ spent time with people whom others shunned: prostitutes, tax collectors, lepers. Religious leaders criticized him for associating with sinners—and then he went out and did it even more.

I started to see that Christ's way was the opposite of my impulse to run away from anyone or anything that was imperfect. I started to notice that, really, I was afraid. My reluctance to commit to imperfect institutions was a fear of my own imperfection. I didn't want to face other people's criticism. By being part of institutions, it felt as if I were assuming all the flaws of those institutions, that I would be "tainted."

But perhaps the Society of Jesus and Catholic Church were the places where I, as an abundantly imperfect human being, needed to be. They were not perfect. But no path was perfect. And these less-than-perfect avenues had led so many people before me to do something great with their lives.

And what was the alternative? Going out on my own? Ha! That would not end well. I needed people to balance me out. I needed a wider perspective than what I had gained from my few years on this planet. If I were to run away and not become a Jesuit and a priest, then I would be free of accusations of clericalism. Criticisms of the Society of Jesus would not apply to me. But it would be so isolating. I might be free of some criticisms but cut off from meaningful ties and a platform for service. Not attaching myself to an institution would have been a recipe for loneliness.

Critical thinking is a gift, but sometimes we abuse the gift and point out only the flaws of any potential commitment. We might think, "That person could be a great spouse, but so many marriages end in divorce. I don't want that to happen to me." We could reason, "I could dive into this creative endeavor and try to share it with the world, but I don't want to be a sellout." If our critical thinking leads us down a road of isolation because of a lack of commitments, then it's time to be critical of our own critical thinking.

Every option is going to be flawed, but a flawed commitment is better than no commitment at all. Institutions such as the family, the church, or a community organization are imperfect—just like us. Running away is tempting, but the only way we build something great is by committing our imperfect selves to imperfect institutions. The worst commitment is no commitment.

Satisficing Is Maximizing

Life is messier than the neat and tidy models that I learned in my economics classes. Traditional economics assumes that people make decisions that will maximize their happiness. This would require us to be perfectly rational and informed. And that makes me laugh. While most of us like to think *we* are rational, it's pretty easy for us to see the irrationality of other people (and for others to see our irrationality).

When COVID-19 hit, there was a run on toilet paper, even though few people with the disease experienced gastrointestinal issues. People soon saw the ridiculousness of it—even if it was still hard to find toilet paper at the store. We made jokes about hoarding toilet paper. But then COVID-19 cases surged months later—and the toilet paper shelves were empty again.

It turns out that we're not always rational and informed. Big shocker, I know. Herbert Simon was an American economist and psychologist who won the Nobel Prize in Economic

Sciences. He argued that maximizing our satisfaction with every decision is not possible. We're limited. We do not have the time and energy to research every single option and know which would make us the happiest. Even if we tried, the time doing the research would be time not enjoying whatever it was we wanted to do. Rather than maximize our utility, Simon advocated "satisficing." Instead of choosing what is *the* best, a "satisficer" settles for what is good enough.

Satisficing rubs many people the wrong way. It seems to run counter to so many of the messages we internalized as children. Our parents and teachers told us, "Do your best." Some high school seniors apply to more than twenty different universities. People submit their résumés to scores of companies. We want to find the best fit. Why would we not seek the best when making life decisions? This is our *life* we are talking about.

A "good enough" mentality also seems to go against people's religious beliefs. Jesus says, "Be perfect, therefore, as your heavenly Father is perfect" (Matthew 5:48). The Ten Commandments do not tell us to honor our parents "most of the time" or to be "good enough" in not coveting. Jesuits talk a lot about the *magis*, the more universal good. We seek the *greater* glory of God, not *a* good option. There is a certain restlessness to the spiritual life. How could a religious person settle for satisficing?

And yet a religious person is still a human person. A limited person. There is no way to know how every possible path will play out. Searching for the "best" option also costs time and emotional energy. If you have to sample the billions of options for a life partner before knowing that you have found "the one," you will be waiting for a very, very long time. Putting pressure on ourselves to choose the perfect path can prevent us from enjoying the journey on which we find ourselves. Sometimes we hold out so long before committing that we never do anything. Even when we eventually commit to something or someone, our indecision can sap our enjoyment. And if we try to maximize our decision but it doesn't turn out well, it's all too easy for us to see something wrong with the *chooser* and not only the choice. We might question our ability to make decisions in the future. We can despair.

According to Eric Barker, "when you calculate all factors of stress, results, and effort, satisficing is actually the method that maximizes."[60] We may not be "perfect," as Christ instructs his followers. Still, we get closer to perfect if we move forward rather than waiting for perfection that is never going to happen. Stopping the quest for "the best" may feel like giving up. However, it actually allows us to give ourselves to something and create the best option.

A note on marriage before we continue. Of course we must discern wisely when choosing a life partner. But if we wait for the "perfect" person, that choice may never come. Married people will testify that most of the perfecting happens over the course of time, over the years of being together. Also, what if you do choose the perfect person for you? It won't be long before that person's imperfections will come to light (yours too). When that happens, will you want to quit the relationship because you think you were mistaken? Do you really want to lay that kind of pressure on your life partner—to be perfect? Do *you* want that kind of pressure?

Feelings Follow Behavior

It can be counterproductive to wait for inspiration to strike before starting a project. Requiring the perfect conditions to begin a task means that we will be waiting a long time. It's possible that we will feel inspired and enthused when tackling a creative project. It's more likely that we will feel bored and hungry and distracted. Did I mention hungry? We might have the perfect conditions to begin a new project. It's more likely that we will have other incomplete projects, overdue bills, and worries about a medical appointment. And did I mention that I was hungry?

Rather than wait for perfect conditions, we need to show up. Every day. And get to work. More often than not, feelings follow behavior. Rather than wait for motivation to fall from the sky, it's progress that will get us motivated. Motivation follows action.

We take care of many tasks that we do not "feel" like accomplishing. Doing laundry is not one of my favorite things in the world. And sometimes I procrastinate and get down to my final pair of clean socks. Still, I'm going to do laundry. That's not a question. For a parent, regardless of how you feel, you're going to feed your child. Most workers are going to do their job regardless of how they feel about it. We don't talk about "farmer's block" or "nurse's block" or "plumber's block." Those things do not exist. People show up and get to work.

Something changes when our work is creative. The get-to-work mentality goes out the window. We lament "writer's block." We pretend that our conditions must be perfect. We think we cannot function unless we are motivated.

Well, perfection ain't gonna happen. We get better only if we allow ourselves to be less-than-perfect along the way. The writer Tim Ferriss talks about the importance of writing "two crappy pages per day."[61] One can always decrapify the pages later. What's deadly is never getting started—or working so infrequently because we're waiting for inspiration.

We can't guarantee the success of our work, but we can guarantee failure by never starting. Getting to spend time on creative endeavors, whether as a job or a hobby, is a privilege. Let's respect the gift. Let's do the work. The "pain" of creating is not the actual pain experienced by a stonemason or an orderly. Even if our conditions are imperfect, we can make do with what we have. Even if we're not feeling motivated in our creative endeavors, we can take some baby steps. Such progress might kick our motivation into gear.

Start Simply—Today

When trying to make some change in our lives, we can make things too complicated. We're better off looking for simple rules with a big impact. Rather than follow a complex diet, many of us could benefit by focusing on one thing: eat more fiber.[62] Fiber is in the good stuff, and it makes you feel full, so you're then less likely to eat the bad stuff. And it's just one rule. Might another diet lead to more weight loss? Most definitely. But if we use up so much willpower trying to follow a complex diet that we give up after a few weeks, then the plan is not very helpful. A normal person stands a chance of following a diet with a single rule. No complex points system. No calorie counting. No list of banned foods. One simple-but-significant rule.

If one wants to start running, she doesn't need to research training programs or find the perfect shoes before she begins. I once ran a marathon in ten-dollar shoes from Walmart. We're better off running around our block with whatever we have rather than wait to get started. Beginning today with something simple is better than delaying until you have the perfect plan. That will never come.

In the spiritual life, we can put pressure on ourselves to use the proper words or the best prayer practice. But maybe a particular prayer style doesn't work for us. That's fine. We could try to have a conversation with God at the same time each day. Oh, and turn off our phones.

Searching for the perfect method is a distraction. If we want to grow in some area of our lives, it's helpful to have a simple-but-significant rule. If we can't follow a method beyond next week, then it's not helpful. We can always improve our routine later, but when we're starting out, we need to lower the pressure on ourselves. Then, in the words of a shoe company that charges more than ten dollars, just do it! That "it" that we "just do" could be minuscule.

Many of us struggle to floss our teeth. We know we should do it. The dentist reminds us that we should do it. "Floss every day" sounds like a simple rule. But that doesn't mean it happens. We may need to lower the expectations even further. Instead of "floss every day," our rule could be "floss one tooth." It's just one tooth. Who can't floss one tooth? We allow ourselves to quit after one. But then if we have flossed one tooth, we think, well, I might as well do the whole mouth. Having a ridiculously low bar might be what we need to make flossing a habit.

Starting small is often the key. Rather than have some elaborate plan for getting stronger, I'm better off starting with one push-up a day. And if I'm already in the push-up position, it's easy to do a few more—perhaps many more. Even if I stop after one, this action is now part of my identity. *I am a push-up person.* And I can deepen that identity and do more tomorrow.

We can always get better over time, but we need to start somewhere. Don't wait to feel motivated. Start today. Just do something small.

Get Your (Crappy) Reps In

A photography professor divided his students into two groups. He told the "quantity" group to take as many pictures as possible and then develop the best ones. He told the "quality" group to be careful and take only the best possible shots. The students submitted their best photos to an independent judge who did not know from which group they came. The judge then selected the best photos, all of which came from the quantity group. Quality came from lowering one's standards, taking a bunch of bad shots, and getting some great ones along the way.[63]

If we want to produce something great, we need to get our reps in. We should not worry about perfection. Mozart, Beethoven, and Bach each composed more than six hundred different pieces.[64] Most of their work is forgettable. But some of those compositions are masterpieces. We might think that there's no way we could ever create something as great as Beethoven's *Ninth Symphony*. But Beethoven did not create something as great as his *Ninth*, 99 percent of the time. He had some duds. But by continually creating, he also produced some works that have stood the test of time.

The Beatles did not become THE BEATLES until they had performed more than a thousand times in the early 1960s. They had to get their reps in. They saw what worked—and what didn't. They got better over time.

The most famous comedians in the world drop in at comedy clubs and try out their new material in front of small audiences. By going through the process of seeing what works when the stakes are low, they know what to cut—and what to use for their Netflix specials.

If we look at innovators in different fields, we often see that the road to quality runs through quantity. The very act of creating, again and again, is what leads to breakthroughs. Most of us do not produce enough. We give up too soon. We become obsessed with trying to refine the few ideas that we have.

It would be nice if we produced only our greatest hits. It would be wonderful to put ourselves out there and never flop. But good luck with that. When it comes to creating, parenting, or priesting, to produce some hits, most of us are going to have some clunkers along the way.

We get to the top of our game only by being less-than-perfect in the process. If we want to create better work, we ought to lower our standards and produce more than we ever have before. Chris Baty advises writers to "lower the bar from 'best-seller' to 'would not make someone vomit.'"[65] If you haven't thrown up while reading this, well, mission accomplished! And if it has made you vomit, please don't tell me. Also, why are you still reading?

Much of what we create will be forgettable, but some of it could be great. And if it's not great? Well, Beethoven also wasn't great most of the time.

Show Your Work

When I look back at some videos I made a few years ago, I cringe. They're pretty bad. But they were necessary. We get better, one crappy rep at a time. If I worried about making every video perfect, then I would hardly produce—and I would be far worse than I am now after many reps.

Alain de Botton has been quoted as saying, "Anyone who isn't embarrassed of who they were last year probably isn't learning enough." One can't fast forward through the journey of imperfection. It will be embarrassing. But if we're putting in the work, we will get better.

Central to getting better is showing your work to others. Tina Fey writes, "You can't be that kid standing at the top of the waterslide, overthinking it. You have to go down the chute. (And I'm from a generation where a lot of people died on waterslides, so this was an important lesson for me to learn.) You have to let people see what you wrote."[66]

It's more comfortable to close ourselves off rather than let others see our imperfection. But then we don't get better. We can't go around or above or under the awkwardness. The only way is through.

I see this with learning languages. It's tempting to study on my own. It's more comfortable than making a fool of myself when speaking with others. But making mistakes—so many mistakes—is a necessary part of the process. That's how we get better. One could use a language-learning app for years and still be unable to speak the language. The only way we reach a point of sounding less-than-ridiculous is by sounding ridiculous along the way.

We could hide. We could choose not to create or put ourselves out there. Or we could step forward and go through the imperfection—and come out better on the other side. Sometimes our work will flop spectacularly. But we learn from that. And we improve. So, share your work. It's good enough. And then do better next time.

What Can I Do Now?

Dearest Fear: Creativity and I are about to go on a road trip together. I understand you'll be joining us, because you always do. I acknowledge that you believe you have an important job to do in my life, and you take your job seriously. Apparently your job is to induce complete panic whenever I'm about to do anything interesting—and, may I say, you are superb at your job. So, by all means, keep doing your job, if you feel you must. But I will also be doing my job on this road trip, which is to work hard and stay focused. And Creativity will be doing its job, which is to remain stimulating and inspiring.[67]

—Elizabeth Gilbert

When have I failed to start something because I was waiting for the conditions to be perfect?

When have I made resolutions that are too big and unsustainable?

When has a fear of imperfection prevented me from doing some good?

In what current situation might I "satisfice" to maximize in the long run?

7

Shut Up and Be a Saint

We might accept the fact that we have to miss out—but that doesn't mean we always accept this quietly. Even if FOMO is not bringing us down, COMO—complaining of missing out—can prevent us from experiencing the freedom of diving into a commitment.

If I started complaining about the boiling point of water, you would likely think me unreasonable, or unbalanced. Water boils at 212°F (100°C) at sea level. You may wish it were lower. It would take less time to make your coffee. But complaining about the boiling point of water would be absurd. The boiling point of water is what it is. We might as well accept it and get on with our lives.

Even if we're fine with the boiling point of water, we complain about other things over which we have the same amount of control—that is, *no* control. We lament the weather. We get outraged by something on social media. We yell when the referee makes a bad call or when the guy from our team misses the buzzer-beater.

Some of those complaints allow us to bond with other people. We talk about the weather because it's a safe topic that can fill awkward silences. We vent about things on social media to people who see things the same way we do and make us feel like we're not alone. We gather around the watercooler and complain about the refs. I hate when a bad call causes my team to lose a game, but I also know that it doesn't *really* matter. Nothing changes in my life except the ability to brag to friends who cheer for the other team.

Sometimes our complaining has more serious consequences. We can spend significant time and energy on issues over which we have no control. This includes things in the past that cannot be changed. We can control how we respond to an event that has happened, but we can't go back in time and change the past. And yet the amount of energy we spend fretting would seem to indicate that we think we can change things.

Sometimes life sucks; we just have to deal with it. But we do anything *but* accept this. We might feel outraged for weeks by something in politics. We go on Twitter rants. We hate-read articles. And at the end of the day, all that energy we spent does absolutely nothing. I'm not going to get the president to change his mind about a decision.

Of course, it might be possible to vote against that person in the next election. We could write a letter or sign a petition expressing our disagreement. We could peacefully protest. But often our options are quite limited. That does not stop us from stewing in frustration. Normally joyful people can get sucked into a political vortex and complain every time you talk with them. It ain't pretty.

When I notice that I'm fired up about something, I try to ask myself *Is this in my sphere of influence?* Well, I *try* to ask myself that question. I have a note on my wall reminding myself to ask that question. I know that I'm a better human being when I ask myself that question. Still, I often don't. I spend an inordinate amount of energy on problems over which I have no influence. I forget that I don't *have* to have an opinion on everything. I complain about the bad weather or the decision made by someone I don't even know. It's not a good way to live.

Most things are outside our sphere of influence. There is a cost to spending our time thinking about them. That politician you disagree with is bad enough. Why give him power over your emotional life as well? Plus, if we're ranting and raving about someone, it's not pleasant for our friends and family members. And just think what we could *do* with all that energy! We could write a thank-you note or tend a garden or read a great book. We're not going to get the time back we spent doomscrolling. No one will say on his deathbed, "I should have tweeted more."

We are human beings, not robots who can turn off our emotions and focus on the task at hand without distraction. And our frustration is a sign that our hearts are working. We actually care. But if we really care about the people and things we *can* influence in a positive way, we can try to spend less time on the things we cannot control. We can work to build something great in our sphere of influence.

Contributing, Not Complaining

Jesus could already run circles around the experts in the temple at the age of twelve. When Mary and Joseph found Jesus in the temple, we learn that "all who heard him were amazed at his understanding and his answers" (Luke 2:47). Still, from that point, "Jesus increased in wisdom and in years" (Luke 2:52). After increasing even more in wisdom, imagine what he was like in his twenties. But he waited. And waited. And waited until he was thirty to start his public ministry.

For decades, he shut up. He took it all in. He observed people and understood the human condition. He "needed no one to testify about anyone; for he himself knew what was in everyone" (John 2:25). I'm often amazed by how Christ answers people in the Gospels. Even when religious leaders try to catch him with a gotcha question, he always has the perfect retort. He waited to start his public ministry until later, but he was probably working on his material for years.

I often get it wrong. I pontificate about something without knowing what I'm talking about. I consume news and commentary that leave me stewing in frustration. I complain—and miss opportunities to make a positive contribution. I shake my fist at the universe instead of trying to grow in wisdom and contribute where I can.

Christ did not remain silent forever. Nor should we. Our world needs saints. But we—or, well, I—could benefit from shutting up a bit more. A little less complaining. A little more contributing.

Serenity Now

The Serenity Prayer works for nearly anyone—even for those who do not normally pray. Alcoholics Anonymous and other twelve-step programs popularized this prayer written by Reinhold Niebuhr: *God, grant me the serenity to accept the things I cannot change, the courage to change the things I can, and the wisdom to know the difference.* Who couldn't use a bit more serenity, courage, and wisdom? It never gets old.

I'm no expert in the courage or wisdom departments, but that first part particularly kills me. Accept the things I cannot change. That means first recognizing that there are many things I cannot change. And then being *okay* with that?

A friend from college was once on a road trip with Fr. Richard Rohr, the Franciscan friar and spiritual writer. At one point, he said, Rohr casually mentioned, "You know, a saint is someone who has forgiven reality."[68] What a great insight—even if I am so far from realizing it.

Ignatian contemplation is a prayer style that uses one's imagination. We picture ourselves in various Gospel scenes and interact with Christ and others from Scripture. My mind often goes all over the place. Sometimes I find myself imagining Christ and the disciples in scenes from my life.

One time, when trying to pray with something from the Bible, I instead saw myself adding coffee grounds to the compost pile outside my house. As I said, my mind goes all over the place. I saw myself trying so hard to contribute my little coffee filter full of grounds. I then saw Jesus show up with a massive dump truck full of the most perfect compost. "Did someone need compost?" he asked. I burst out laughing.

I try so hard, but from a Christian perspective, my effort is a drop in the ocean compared to God's activity. We talk a lot about cooperating with God's grace and even being a co-creator with God. And it's true. Even something as small as adding coffee grounds to a compost pile can be an effort to care for God's creation. But let's not forget his massive dump truck. We're called to be saints—not messiahs. We don't have to be the Savior of the World. That job is filled.

So, how do we go about shutting up and being saints? How do we stop complaining about the bad things that happen to us and contribute in the ways we can? How do we accept the things we cannot change and have the courage to change the things we can? There's no silver bullet, but what follow are four helpful strategies.

1) Try a different frame.

I sometimes tell myself, "*Ugh*, I should work out." At other moments, I say "Okay! It's time to get strong and feel great afterward." Both statements are true. I should exercise. And when I do, I feel great. But what I choose to focus on makes an enormous difference in my attitude and actions. I can choose the frame through which I see a particular set of events.

If I'm only thinking about the duty to exercise, I'm not very motivated. I might work out but with a grudge. But seeing a workout as a lifeless obligation is not the only option. One could see a workout as a way to have more days to spend with grandchildren. Another person could work out to get back at the childhood bully who made fun of him for being weak. A different person could see it as a way to get an amazing endorphin rush.

There is more than one way of viewing things. Marcus Aurelius writes, "How good it is when you have roast meat or suchlike foods before you, to impress on your mind that this is the dead body of a fish, this is the dead body of a bird or pig."[69] It's difficult to resist a juicy steak. It's a lot easier to resist some dead animal. "Juicy steak" is not the only lens. We have options.

If we can't stop complaining about our current circumstances, it's time to try a different frame. If I lose my job, I could focus on the lost salary. I could fret about my uncertain future. Or I could see how I got fifty hours of my week back and have the chance to try something new. A new lens does not make our problems go away, but we can see some opportunities, too.

Crappy things happen to us. Life can be cruel. But there are different ways to view a situation. Some are more helpful than others.

2) Don't get mad. Get curious.

I grew up in Iowa. I am well versed in Midwestern niceness. Some might call it passive aggression. Midwesterners can detest something, but if you ask us what we think about it, we'll say, "Hmm, that's interesting."

Southerners can do something similar. "Bless your heart" may really mean, "You are an absolute moron. I cannot stand you. I hope you step in dog poop." Tomayto, tomahto.

My Midwestern soul cringes when I hear a New Yorker telling me what he really feels, but I recognize that Midwestern passive aggression comes with its own problems. Still, a stance of "Hmm, that's interesting" might be what we need.

Levels of interpersonal trust in the United States are at worrisome levels. Support for interracial marriage has skyrocketed in recent decades, but support for "interpolitical" marriage has plummeted. In 1958, 72 percent of Americans said they would not care if their child married someone of the opposite political party. That number has dropped to 45 percent.[70] The divides run deeper than differing ideas about tax policy. It's hard for us to imagine a child of ours with one of *those people*.

It often seems that we live in different galaxies—or at least different media ecosystems. Still, many of us have family members who see the world differently and vote for the other political party. It can make for an awkward Thanksgiving dinner.

The next time we're frustrated with the views of another, instead of getting upset, we can try to get curious. It's impossible to feel mad and curious at the same time. In lieu of frustration, we can aim for fascination and explore how people from the same family or community can see things so differently.

If we pretend that we're Scooby Doo and try to solve the mystery of how we disagree so much, the tension goes away. It's more fun imagining you're a cartoon character than arguing with your uncle at the dinner table after you've both had one too many. Plus, to solve the mystery, we have to listen to people. Now, *that's* interesting.

3) Do some good in the world.

Not only can shutting up help us become saints but trying to be saints can help us shut up. Trying to do some good in the world might be exactly what we need to quiet our minds and quit complaining. My running coach used to tell us that it was fine to have butterflies in your stomach before a race. Just get them flying in the right direction. It's normal to get frustrated. We just need to get that frustration flying in the right direction.

Some outlets for our anger are better than others. I could get behind the wheel and honk at any idiot driving too slowly. I could also honk at any maniac driving too fast. I could honk at anyone else on the road who is not going at exactly the speed that I think they should be going. Alternatively, I could use all the energy I have for a productive purpose.

In Dostoevsky's *The Brothers Karamazov*, a "lady of little faith" comes to the elder Zosima and asks for advice. He tells her, "Try to love your neighbors actively and tirelessly. The more you succeed in loving, the more you'll be convinced of the existence of God and the immortality of your soul."[71] Faith can lead one to action, but action can also lead one to faith.

Zosima's advice is relevant when we're frustrated and cannot calm our monkey minds. We can try to quit navel gazing and do some good for another person. Maybe we're furious about something in the news. We can think about it constantly. But if we go out of ourselves, we see that the vast majority of people are thinking about other things. They're focused on picking up their kids from soccer practice and making dinner. They're preparing a presentation for work. They're worried about a friend with cancer. And they could use some help.

In both Christianity and the Western philosophical tradition, freedom is not doing whatever the heck we want. St. Paul writes in his Letter to the Galatians, "For freedom Christ has set us free" (5:1). It sounds redundant at first, but Paul is distinguishing between two kinds of freedom: freedom from and freedom for. Most of the talk of "freedom," at least in the United States, is freedom *from*. But that's not the whole picture. Freedom is also *for* service.

The Catholic catechism states, "The more one does what is good, the freer one becomes."[72] This is not just a pious platitude relevant for practicing Catholics. It's backed up by research. According to Martin Seligman, one of the pioneers in positive psychology, "We scientists have found that doing a kindness produces the single most reliable momentary increase in well-being of any exercise we have tested."[73] Doing something good for another person not only helps others. It helps *us*.

And if you do not feel like doing something good for another person? Well, do it anyway. *Particularly* when you're not feeling like it, do it anyway. When we are in a state of desolation, doing something good for others does not come easily. But that's when we need to do it even more. It's a surefire way to fight the desolation. Stopping our complaining not only helps us become saints (and more pleasant to be around). Trying to be saints can also help us to shut up and stop complaining. ·

4) Laugh at yourself.

Complaining is about as attractive as talking with your mouth full, but it's hard to stop ourselves. If we can't shut up and are going to make some noise anyway, we might as well laugh. We can treat our complaining selves like that friend who shows up at your place and doesn't take the hint that you want some time to yourself. There he is again. Rather than get frustrated with yourself for getting so frustrated, it's a lot better to laugh. Laughter takes the power away. The more we laugh, the less the frustration has a grip on us.

People who laugh are often the most courageous. In *Live Not by Lies*, Rod Dreher highlights the work of Fr. Tomislav Kolaković. This Jesuit formed small Christian communities that resisted the Soviet regime in the former Czechoslovakia. Silvester Krčméry was one of the men Kolaković mentored. The Soviets arrested this young doctor in 1951. While sitting in the police car, Krčméry thought, "There could not be anything more beautiful than to lay down my life for God," and immediately burst into laughter. His *captors* did not find it amusing, but Krčméry joyfully realized that not even prison could shake him.[74]

Dr. Gordon Livingston was a best-selling author and psychiatrist who helped many people in grief. He wrote, "Of all the forms of courage, the ability to laugh is the most profoundly therapeutic."[75] Laughter is not a sign of weakness. It's often a form of strength. It feels pretty great, too!

Even if their depictions look quite serious, many of the saints did not take themselves too seriously. Ignatius often looks stern in paintings. This has led one friend to say that he doesn't fear God on Judgment Day, but he does fear Ignatius! But there was more to the guy. St. Ignatius would tell jokes, pull people's ears, and even dance a jig to try to cheer a person up. He once told a novice, "Laugh, my son, and be joyful in the Lord, for a religious has no reason to be sad and has a thousand reasons to rejoice."[76] The writer Anne Lamott has called laughter "carbonated holiness."[77] We might *think* that holy people are super serious all the time. Many of them are having a blast—especially when laughing at themselves.

Making commitments, which will be the focus of the final section of this book, bakes many of these strategies into the cake. Having a family means living with people who inevitably see things from different perspectives. Knowing that people rely on us pushes us to break out of our social media silos and do some good in the world. Taking on responsibility and (inevitably) failing means that there will be plenty of opportunities to laugh at ourselves. We still have work to do. We can't be on autopilot. Still, making serious commitments makes shutting up and being a saint far more likely.

What Can I Do Now?

If I didn't have kids there's a 5 percent chance that I'd be doing something more radical in pursuit of sainthood; there's a 95 percent chance that I'd just be a more persistent sinner, a more selfish person, because no squalling infant or tearful nine-year-old is there to force me to live for her and not myself.[78]

—Ross Douthat

In what situation(s) have I spent time and energy getting frustrated about something over which I had absolutely no control?

What's in my sphere of influence? What's not?

In what areas of my life could I complain less and contribute more?

How can I get curious about a recent situation that has frustrated me? Can I laugh?

SAYING YES

8

We Like What's Easy.
We Love What's Hard.

The fear of missing out feeds our desire for freedom—to enjoy what we want when we want. And that sort of "freedom" will move us toward what is easy, immediate, and comfortable. FOMO will move us away from what is difficult, what requires time and long-term thinking, and what is not always comfortable or pleasant.

If I invite you to my home for a meal, I *could* pour you a bowl of cereal. I *could* microwave a TV dinner or prepare some instant ramen. But that would be so wrong! I would want to do more. Preparing a meal is a way of showing that I care. Giving no effort and offering low-quality fare would not be the appropriate way to honor the presence of a guest. It would be easy, but it would not be meaningful.

We may like what's easy, but we experience deeper satisfaction from those things that require a personal investment. It's comfortable to consume a video or an article that someone else produced. It's harder, but more satisfying, to create content that others can enjoy. For students, there's a difference between doing enough to get by and fully investing oneself in writing a paper or preparing a project. It may not even make a difference in one's final grade, but *we* know the difference between phoning it in and mastering the material. Checking sports or one's social media feed at work may be enjoyable, but wasting time on someone else's dime does not make us proud.

Parenting is the best example of this dynamic. It's not pleasant to get up throughout the night to feed one's baby or fail to sleep while worrying about one's teenager, but parenting is a profound source of meaning. A cat is easier to raise than a Catherine; a dog takes less work than a Doug. While it might be satisfying to see one's pet be a "good boy," it does not compare with seeing one's child grow up to become a good person. Parenting involves countless sacrifices—and unparalleled satisfaction.

Longing for Hardship

We complain about being busy, but the truth is, we love being busy—at least when we are busy with meaningful endeavors. When we are swamped with work and worn down by family responsibilities, it's easy to think how nice it would be to get away from it all. Sometimes we talk as if the fewer responsibilities we had, the better life would be. But that's simply not the case.

We might complain about all that we need to do, but it's far better than not having enough to do. And *we* are better for it. Engaging in generative activity is better than taking the easy road and feeling that we're not needed.

A life without responsibilities is the equivalent of cotton candy. It's colorful and fun when you're young, but it fails to satisfy. Human beings need some hardship in their lives, something to overcome. If everything were provided for us, we would have no sense of accomplishment. We long to feel that we are necessary.

The great majority of people throughout history were not lacking in challenges to overcome. Finding enough food for one's family and protecting them from enemies were opportunities to accomplish something meaningful. We *homo sapiens* emerged on this green earth 200,000 years ago. We are the descendants of those who survived plagues, wars, famines, and natural disasters. We've inhabited wildly different climates—and did so long before central heating and air conditioning. We learned to hunt lions and tigers and bears.

But, oh my, we seem to have lost something. We have replaced many of the challenges that gave life meaning with activities that do not matter. Far fewer people today fight for their tribe or nation in war. Instead, we fight each other in the comments section. Most of us do not struggle to find food, but we struggle to maintain the perfect lawn. We do not worry about the Black Death, but we worry about getting enough likes on social media.

In his book *Tribe*, Sebastian Junger recounts how many combat veterans come back home and miss the deep bonds they formed with their fellow soldiers and the sense of mission they had on the battlefield. They may now be free from danger, but their lives can also feel free of meaning. Junger writes, "Humans don't mind hardship, in fact they thrive on it; what they mind is not feeling necessary. Modern society has perfected the art of making people not feel necessary."[79] We can drown in comfort while lacking a sense of purpose.

So many things in the world have gotten better. Global life expectancy has increased by more than thirty years since 1950. Far more people live free of oppression than ever before. Losing a child has gone from a common occurrence to a rare tragedy. Despite what may be apparent from news headlines, people today are far less likely to live in extreme poverty or die because of violence than in any other era in human history. These are all wonderful things.

But life is more than quality-of-life indicators. We could be safe, physically healthy, and educated—but also quite miserable. We still have the human longing to feel that our lives matter. When our basic needs are taken care of, we need to seek out additional challenges rather than have those challenges seek *us*.

And what we choose to seek matters. Challenges vary in their level of meaning. We could challenge ourselves to finish every episode of every season of a show on Netflix. We could eat as much as possible at the all-you-can-eat buffet. We could rack up one-night stands. Or we could embrace meaningful challenges. We could take up a craft—gardening, woodworking, beekeeping, whatever—and become great at it. We could commit to a fellow imperfect person and make it work, even when it's not easy. *Especially* when it's not easy. We could welcome new life into the world and provide for the next generations. At the end of our lives, we would look back and remember how we gave ourselves to building relationships and institutions. We're not going to remember what we posted on social media.

While it's not always pleasant, we long to make sacrifices for the things that matter. It's not that we are gluttons for punishment. Rather, we want to be part of something larger than ourselves. Giving of ourselves can be uncomfortable, but we will rest more comfortably knowing that we chose what's meaningful over what's easy.

Lonely Comfort

The Spanish word *aislar* can be translated as either "to iso-late" or "to insulate." In an effort to *insulate* ourselves from discomfort, we can often *isolate* ourselves in the process. Moving to a bigger place might mean more bathrooms and storage space, but that same place might require a longer commute and thus less time with family and friends. We're more likely to remember the vacation when we were freezing in a tent than we are the one when we stayed in a nice hotel room that looked like every other nice hotel room in the world.

In college, I lived with 330 other men in a dormitory built in 1931. The bedrooms were tiny. Our roommates were assigned at random. Our bathrooms were communal. And the only room in the building with air conditioning was the chapel. (Very subtle, Notre Dame, very subtle.) It was not possible to isolate yourself when there were so many men living on top of one another. Many of the best times with friends happened after a spontaneous encounter in the hallway. It often was not quiet. Roommates snored. Parties took place down the hall until two in the morning. It was not comfortable, but it was memorable.

I go back to campus now, and I'm astounded at just how nice it is. That 1931 building has been renovated. New dormitories have much bigger rooms. People see air conditioning as essential. There are gorgeous new spaces for students to relax and study in. There's more space in general, even though the student body has not increased. There are fewer chances to rub elbows because those elbows are spread out over a much greater area. It's surely more comfortable, but that does not translate into meaningful interactions. Something can be lost in the process.

Life Is More than Efficiency

I've lived on four continents. I'm quite familiar with different cultures and languages. Still, the most foreign experience of my life happened in Chicago, my adult home. What was this strange experience? A baby shower. It was a different world, with its own rituals. All the women seemed to know the rules. I was clueless. It was a beautiful way to show support to the expectant mother. I just didn't *get* it.

One coworker knit a baby blanket as a gift for the new mother. She spent seventy hours on this thing! Seventy hours! I kept thinking about all the books I could read in that amount of time. I was even more astounded when I saw that she spent seventy hours on something that you could buy for about ten dollars on Amazon. Obviously, I'm using a different logic. And I'm an inconsiderate jerk.

Knitting a baby blanket was not a utilitarian exercise. It was a labor of love. It was a powerful symbol that showed how this coworker cared for the new mother. It would be easier and cheaper to order something online, but the act of knitting was an exercise in meaning. At times it makes sense to do what's easy and comfortable. But not all the time. We long to give of ourselves and sacrifice our time and energy for the important people in our lives.

Around the middle of the twentieth century, Pillsbury had a problem. Their cake mixes were not selling well. They had made things easy for the potential cake baker. All one had to do was add water. Every other ingredient was already in the mix. Still, sales were rather stagnant. Why would people not want to buy something that made it so easy for them to bake a cake at home?

Eventually, Pillsbury fixed their cake mix problem and made sales skyrocket. How? They made things harder. They removed the dried eggs from the cake mix and required bakers to add the eggs themselves. Far more people started buying the cake mixes when they had to do *more* work.

How could this be? Perhaps the cakes tasted better when one used fresh eggs, but there's more to the story. Pillsbury realized that making a cake is not about efficiency. We bake cakes for special occasions. It's a way of showing we care. If I only have to add water, it doesn't "count." There's no labor of love because there's hardly any labor! If I at least add the eggs, I'm more involved in the process. I feel that I have made a contribution. It shows that I care.

"Welcome" Isn't Enough

Being attracted to something that asks more of us is not unique to cake mixes. Many religious groups that are growing are those that ask a lot of their adherents. Rodney Stark and William Bainbridge call this "high-tension religion" in their book *A Theory of Religion*.[80] "Low-tension" groups that do not provide much of a contrast with the surrounding culture are more likely to experience decline. Religious groups that ask much of their members often experience high levels of commitment.

The Church of Jesus Christ of Latter-Day Saints is an example of a high-tension religious group that has seen significant growth. They ask a lot of their followers. There are high expectations when it comes to tithing and sexual morality. They encourage young men to go on mission for two years. And one cannot even drink coffee! Still, their rapid growth may not be *despite* such high expectations; it may in part be *because* of such high expectations.

One can find many examples of this dynamic at play within Catholicism. Many of the women's religious orders experiencing growth in the United States today require the habit and are in high tension with the surrounding culture. Most low-tension congregations of sisters are seeing significant declines. Young women might think that if they are going to enter religious life, they might as well go all in and live a radically different lifestyle. Otherwise, why would they take vows of poverty, chastity, and obedience?

It's noteworthy to see where young adult Catholics go to Mass. At many Catholic parishes in the United States, one sees an almost total lack of twentysomethings. A parish may sing "All Are Welcome" as its gathering song. They may have greeters with smiling faces at the door. But that does not guarantee that young people will show up. If it's a Mass in Latin with all the smells and bells, however, one is more likely to see many young adults. Traditionalist Catholics are a minority, but they are a notable percentage of the young Catholics who go to church every week.

Personally, I prefer Mass in a language I actually speak. I like kind people at the door welcoming me as I come in. But welcome isn't enough. I can get "welcome" just about anywhere. I'm also welcome to eat brunch at the restaurant around the block, but I'm not going to give my life for eggs

Benedict. We long for something greater than ourselves. We desire that which is different and meaningful and beautiful. I might know that I am welcome at a particular church, but if it doesn't feel different from the rest of my life, if it does not ask much of me, then I might wonder, *What's the point?* It's a lot easier to sleep in.

Welcomed and Wanted

I taught at a Jesuit high school for two years in Tanzania. One of my favorite parts of the experience was teaching young people who *believed*. Their faith inspired me regularly.

I later saw some of my former students when they visited the United States through an exchange program. The Tanzanian students stayed with host families from the Jesuit high school in Boston. Their stories were illuminating.

One former student talked about going to Mass with her host family. This student was appalled that the priest thanked the congregation for coming to the liturgy. Someone from the US might think that a word of thanks was a nice gesture. My former student was having none of it.

"This is our Creator!" she said. "The *least* we can do is go and worship! I do not want to be thanked just for going to church!"

She has a point. A common temptation for churches experiencing a decline is to try to make things easier for people. They may hint that they don't *really* expect you to be there every week. They may choose not to highlight the hard teachings of the faith. In addition to being unfaithful to the Gospel, such a strategy is often ineffective. The fact that so many young people have left the church may not be because the Church asked too much of young people. Rather, it's partly because we haven't asked enough. We have failed to put before them the adventure of a life with God.

In *Divine Renovation*, Fr. James Mallon advocates that parishes practice "high welcome and high expectation." These things don't have to be in conflict. Mallon writes that having both high welcome and high expectation is much better than saying, "You are most welcome here, and, by the way, we don't expect anything from you at all."[81] We want to be welcomed. We also want to be wanted. We want to give our lives to something meaningful. This can take different forms. Parishes might expect their faithful to join small Christian communities or participate in service projects or engage in Eucharistic adoration. Vibrant churches ask much of their followers.

A Life Worth Living

There is a certain level of friction in making a commitment. It's not as relaxing to volunteer on the weekend as it is to sleep in or watch football. Organizing a regular book group or Bible study requires time and energy. Changing a career or committing oneself to a person for life involves a huge adjustment to one's routine.

Often, the friction is too great. We stay with the status quo. We stick with what's easy. We continue with what we know.

But if we just get over the hump, we can find far more meaning on the other side. Volunteering not only makes other people's lives better but also makes *our* lives better. Being an active part of a community takes work, but being part of something larger than ourselves is deeply satisfying. Our lives take on a different texture when we are responsible for others. We may like the easier path, but we often don't *love* the easier path. Comfort is pleasant, but comfort isn't what makes life worth living.

What Can I Do Now?

Not everything that's hard is good of course, but almost everything good is hard. Think about all the things you're good at. There was a time when you weren't good at them, right? When they were hard. But you worked at it. Despite feeling deficient and frustrated, and fighting the urge to quit, you saw a glimpse of goodness, you clawed out a bit of progress, you felt a glimmer of confidence, and you chose to keep at it. To keep pushing. And you grew from the fight against the resistance. Even more, you found something on the other side of it all—a you that you realized you didn't entirely know and had possibly never met. You learned something incredibly valuable about yourself: you're capable of more than you know.[82]

—Ryan Holiday

When have efforts to insulate myself from discomfort ever isolated me from others?

When have I chosen what was meaningful over what was easy? How do I see that situation now?

In what parts of my life do I make a significant contribution to a shared enterprise? Are there ways I might make a deeper contribution?

We often look for the easier path (an email instead of a handwritten note, the elevator instead of the stairs, or mere attendance instead of a leadership role), but how might I benefit from making something in my life *harder*?

9

Shouldn't I Wait Until I'm Certain?

A Jesuit trying to determine how best to serve once asked Mother Teresa to pray that he might have certainty. "No," she said.

Wait, what?! the Jesuit must have thought. *I just asked Mother Teresa to pray for me, and she said* no?

Mother Teresa told the Jesuit that he was clinging to certainty. He had to let go. When the Jesuit objected and said that she always seemed to have certainty, Mother Teresa laughed and said that she had never experienced certainty but that she had trust. And she would pray that he trust God. There's nothing quite like a spiritual butt kicking from Mother Teresa.

Sometimes God will confirm a decision by giving us overwhelming certainty. We get knocked off our horse. From the core of our being, we *know*. But that's rare. Instead, we need to look for many data points from God that paint a picture. That picture may be fuzzy. It will probably look more like an Impressionist painting than a photo taken on the latest smartphone. We wish we had greater clarity. But we still have to trust. We have to commit.

Decide Anyway

There was a set of "paradoxical commandments" on the wall of Mother Teresa's home for children in Calcutta. There's a good chance you've seen them on social media: "People are often unreasonable, irrational, and self-centered. Forgive them anyway. If you are kind, people may accuse you of self-ish, ulterior motives. Be kind anyway. . . ."

We could add another such commandment: "We may never have absolute certainty when making a decision. Decide anyway."

To an outside observer, Mother Teresa seemed like a woman who had certainty. She committed herself to a radical way of discipleship that inspired the world. In reality, Mother Teresa often did not have certainty. After her death, we learned that she had experienced decades of spiritual dryness. But she decided anyway. She trusted in God.

We might think that we should wait until we have certainty before committing ourselves to a certain person or project or place. We could be waiting for a long time. That certainty will probably never arrive.

When considering a commitment, we need to do our homework. We must get our hands dirty, try out different experiences, and gather data. We need to pay attention to what makes us come alive and how our decisions might affect others. Still, even after serious discernment, we will rarely have certainty. But we must decide anyway.

Ready, Aim, Fire

Rather than take an approach of "ready, aim, fire," some people rush into a decision and instead "*fire*, ready, aim." Hold up, Partner. We often need to slow things down, take the pressure off, and gather more data before deciding. This is our life here. We don't want to rush into things blindly.

At other times, we have plenty of data, but what we really need is courage. It's easy for us to "ready, aim, aim, aim"—without making a decision. We tell ourselves we need to gather more information. Maybe we're just afraid of making a commitment. It's possible that we need more patience. It's probable that we need more courage.

I received some mixed messages during my first discernment event with the Jesuits. One Jesuit advised us to take our time with the discernment process. "There's no rush," he said. Another Jesuit told us to "strike while the iron's hot" and "don't wimp out!" There's no rush, but strike while the iron's hot. Take your time, but don't wimp out. How do we make sense of such seemingly contradictory messages? There's some wisdom in both pieces of advice.

Sometimes, there is no rush. A young person has her whole life ahead of her. She needs some life experience before being able to make any significant long-term commitment. It's fine if she does not have the perfect answer when an older person asks her what she wants to do with her life.

In some situations, time is not an issue. Let's say you're considering buying something. Despite hearing about a "limited-time offer," we often have *plenty* of options for buying something. If we do not take this offer, there will undoubtedly be another "limited-time offer" whenever we're ready to make a purchase. Never underestimate the power of capitalism to sell you anything that you could dream of—and many things you couldn't. (*Pumpkin spice hand sanitizer? Macaroni and cheese ice cream?*) There's no rush.

At other times, we *do* need to strike while the iron is hot. Windows of opportunity can close. Our health will diminish. Future responsibilities may prevent us from doing some of the things that are possible to us now. Each day we get closer to the end of our lives.

In my work with men discerning religious life, perpetual delayers are the most painful to watch. It hurts to see a great guy discern that God is not calling him to be a Jesuit, but I'm happy for him when he confidently embarks on a different path. There are other men who express interest in the Jesuits but quickly discover that this is not a great fit for them. That's fine. Most people are not called to this life. The most difficult cases are the guys for whom it seems that God is calling them to this Jesuit life. But they're afraid. They want to make sure. They want more time. And they drift. Their sense of calling fizzles. They often end up not committing to anything.

The uncommitted life is the unremarkable life. That doesn't mean we fail to discern. We must do our homework and see how we can best give glory to God. But then we need to trust God and take a leap. We're not getting any younger. We need to ready, aim . . . and then fire!

You're Probably Too Timid

It's possible to be too hasty in making decisions, but most of us are too hesitant. Steven Levitt of *Freakonomics* fame found 20,000 people who were considering some change in their lives. They were discerning everything from getting a tattoo to quitting their job to starting a family. They agreed to flip a coin. Heads meant making the change. Tails meant staying put. Even though there was no penalty for not following through, most of the people who got heads went ahead and made the change they were considering. This invitation to flip a coin is what they needed to get over the hump and change something in their lives.

Six months later, those who made the change were significantly happier than those who had stayed with the status quo. Levitt says this suggests that most of us are biased against making significant changes in our lives, even when such changes would benefit us.[83] Most of us are too timid.

Recalibrating our default setting could help. Rather than ask ourselves, "Should I do this or not?" we could ask, "Knowing that I'm usually better off making bold decisions, why *wouldn't* I go ahead with this?" There may be good reasons not to make the change we are considering. And we should not be reckless. Please don't try to sue me if you get a face tattoo—because #YOLO ("you only live once")—and then regret it later. Still, most of us could use a bit more boldness.

There is a popular narrative that people in the United States are increasingly mobile. People think that we move from place to place without the same rootedness as before. It's a myth. We do have our mobile *devices*. But the idea that Americans are moving more today than they did in the past?

It's not at all true. In 1950, roughly one in five Americans changed homes each year. Today? It's one in ten.[84]

There could be some positive aspects to our decreasing mobility. People might live closer to their friends and family. Kids might be able to see their grandparents more often. Fewer people moving may also indicate higher levels of security. It may be that fewer people are being *forced* to move.

But there are worrisome signs too. It's not like we're moving less so that we're building robust families and communities at higher rates. Many of us don't even know our neighbors. People in the United States under the age of thirty are not only less likely to relocate for a career but also much less likely to start businesses. The trend of moving less matches up with other trends indicating more risk-averse behavior.

Most of us could use some more boldness. Books like Tyler Cowen's *The Complacent Class* and Ross Douthat's *The Decadent Society* illustrate how we seem to be losing our mojo. Peter Thiel famously complained, "We wanted flying cars, instead we got 140 characters." That was in reference to the original limit of a tweet. Perhaps he was too pessimistic. Now we can use 280 characters. Huzzah! Despite the doubling of the length of a tweet, the frontier spirit of Americans has been declining for decades.

Don't Wait for the 100 Percent

The example of one of the boldest—and richest—businessmen can be instructive. In 1994, Amazon founder Jeff Bezos had a lucrative job at a hedge fund. Most reasonable people would have told him that it would be crazy to leave such a situation. But he saw that the Web was growing by leaps and bounds. He could not stop thinking about trying to build a bookstore online. He recognized that if he never tried it out, he would regret it later in life.[85] Well, he tried, and it seems to have worked out for him just fine.

Decisions involve uncertainty. Waiting for 100 percent confidence will often mean waiting forever. In a 2016 shareholder letter, Jeff Bezos wrote, "Most decisions should probably be made with somewhere around 70% of the information you wish you had. If you wait for 90%, in most cases, you're probably being slow."[86] Commentators have referred to this as the "70 percent rule." Now, cutthroat competition with other retailers does not influence most of our daily decisions. Still, even in our personal lives, waiting until we're certain may mean missing out on windows of opportunity that can close. The "70 percent rule" helps us avoid extremes. We do not make important decisions based on our initial instincts alone, but we also do not wait for certainty. We fight "analysis paralysis" and make decisions.

Sins of Omission

"Sins of commission" get most of the attention, but "sins of omission" are far more common. For a sports fan, trades that end in disaster for one of the teams are like a bad accident on the road. I cannot look away! Sports fans love to ridicule teams that swing for the fences but fall on their faces.

What's more common is that teams do not take a big chance. They worry that sports fans like me will criticize them, so they do not rock the boat. But only one team wins the championship every year. To get there, a team cannot play it safe the whole time. They must be smart. It helps if you have a generational talent like Tom Brady or LeBron James on your team. But for a team to win it all, they must also be bold.

Bronnie Ware was a songwriter who worked for years in palliative care. She wrote a blog post in which she outlined five common regrets people expressed near the end of their lives. That post went viral and led to a memoir entitled *The Top Five Regrets of the Dying*. It has been translated into more than twenty-five languages. According to Ware, the number one regret of the dying is, "I wish I'd had the courage to live a life true to myself, not the life others expected of me."[87] Recognizing how we have not pursued our dreams eats away at us.

We are more likely to regret the things we did not do than the things we did. If a new project fails miserably, that will hurt. But at least we tried. If we ask out the person of our dreams, it's not pleasant to be rejected. But at least we went for it. At the end of the day—or the end of our lives—it's much harder to sit with all the things we did not try because we were afraid. If we tried and failed, we can come up with all sorts of reasons why things didn't work out. We're masters at rationalization. But if we did not try at all because we were afraid, then there's no one to blame but ourselves.

Whether we have days or decades remaining on this earth, we can make changes in our lives today. Steve Jobs gave the 2005 commencement address at Stanford University. He had already been diagnosed with cancer at that time. He told the graduates, "Remembering that I'll be dead soon is the most important tool I've ever encountered to help me make the big choices in life."[88]

Jobs had to confront his own mortality because of his health condition, but his advice echoes an ancient tradition relevant for people of any health status: *Memento mori*. Remember your death. It sounds morbid, particularly in a culture that seems to ignore death as much as possible. But when we regularly contemplate our death, we remember how we want to live.

Reaching the Double Negative

I learned early on not to use a double negative in English. I later discovered that double negatives are illuminating when making decisions.

In many languages, it's normal to use a double negative. You might say, "*No hay ningún problema*" in Spanish or "*Non c'è nessun problema*" in Italian. In standard English, however, we don't use a double negative. Saying, "There isn't no problem" is, in fact, a problem!

At least most of the time. Sometimes we have to throw the grammar rules out the window. When discerning God's will for your life, pay attention when you reach the point of the double negative, when you find yourself saying "I cannot *not* do this." That's a strong indication that you need to cross the Rubicon and follow the path you are considering—or affirm the path that seems to have been chosen for you.

I came to a point in college when this idea of being a Jesuit would not go away. It was an itch that I had to scratch. I could not know with certainty that this is what God was calling me to, but I knew enough that I had to take the next step. I could not *not* do this.

The "Oh, Crap" Test

What we fear doing most might be what we most need to do. I suspect God is calling a guy to religious life when I hear him say something like "This scares the hell out of me, but I can't *shake* it."

It's normal to feel some resistance to giving up family life, independence, and social approval. Those are good things. And, let's be honest, being a priest or religious brother is not exactly normal. Most people do not take vows of poverty, chastity, and obedience. One does not decide on a whim that he's going to become a Jesuit. But when he still can't get the idea out of his head—and when there's a joyful excitement that accompanies the idea—that's a good sign that this life is for him. He needs to push past the fear.

When we're starting to identify God's will for our lives, it's pretty common to think, "Oh, crap—really, God? You're asking me to do *this*? Why can't I do something normal or easy?"

And yet, if something is really of God, it's also going to be life giving. We might think, "Oh, crap, really? And yet . . . this is exciting. And I can't stop thinking about it!"

This oh-crap feeling is different from the gnawing anxiousness that is characteristic of an option that is not in sync with God. If something is coming from God, it will click with our holiest desires. We will feel a sense of enlargement.

We may still wonder whether God got the right person, but there tends to be an underlying joy, even if the new path will turn our lives upside down.

Push Past the Fear

The most repeated command in the Gospels is not about sex or money or religious practice. Rather, it's about not being afraid. What does the angel Gabriel tell Mary at the Annunciation? "Do not be afraid." What does Jesus tell Simon when he calls him on the seashore? "Do not be afraid." What does the angel tell the women when they find the empty tomb? "Do not be afraid." There are *hundreds* of instances in the Bible in which we read some version of "Do not be afraid."

We know this is easier said than done. Fear is the thing that usually gets in the way of good people doing God's will. Most of us do not struggle to avoid robbing a bank or building a golden calf. But we fail to do a lot of the good we could do because of fear. We don't speak up when we ought to because we worry it could be misconstrued. We don't reach out to the person who's going through a tough time because it could be awkward. We don't volunteer because it could be uncomfortable—and it's a lot easier to stay home and watch videos on YouTube. The next time we hesitate to do something that intimidates us, we can ask ourselves a weighted question: *Knowing that fear is the biggest obstacle to holiness, why* wouldn't *I go ahead with this thing that makes me afraid?* It can be quite clarifying.

Even the Best Decisions Have Drawbacks

Sometimes I meet a guy who worries that if he becomes a priest, he will be lonely. He probably will experience loneliness as a priest, but loneliness is not unique to the priesthood. That same person could be just as lonely if he got married. We should not disregard an option simply because there is something human about it.

On Halloween every year, my college friends share the most adorable pictures of their kids in costumes. My phone buzzes throughout the evening with photos of yet another cute kid. I felt sad the first few years this happened. I don't have children of my own. I felt as if I was missing out. I later realized that they shared pictures of the adorable costumes but didn't share pictures of the temper tantrums or poopy diapers (thank God).

Sometimes we think that if we make the right choice, then things will be perfect. That's not the case this side of heaven. There are always downsides, even with the best decisions. Getting married and having kids may mean you can't watch sports with your friends quite as often. But family life is a wonderful vocation. Taking a job in a different city that will utilize your skills and pay you much more probably makes sense. And it will also require saying goodbye to friends and your favorite neighborhood joint in the place you've called home.

Even the best job is going to have unpleasant aspects. Maybe it pays well but includes a lot of travel. Maybe the hours are great but filled with too many meetings. Maybe you love your boss, but your colleague down the hall can be a jerk.

We resist diving into a commitment because of the potential drawbacks, but every commitment has drawbacks. Discernment is always between good options in the real world—not utopia. An important question to ask ourselves is, *Compared to what?* Sometimes we're considering a good-but-flawed option and comparing it to perfection. It's not a fair comparison. We have to say yes to all that comes with a decision—including the downsides—and then experience the joy that comes from deep commitment.

We should never underestimate the power of human stupidity. We can all think of times we've rushed into bone-headed decisions. But more often, we lack courage. What have you done lately that scares you? If you can't think of anything, you may be playing it too safe. That thing that scares you to death might be exactly what you need to do.

What Can I Do Now?

Years and scores of thousands of dollars are spent getting degrees and certificates that fundamentally don't cultivate people's courage such that they can thrive in the professional world. . . . The reality is that your smartest next step is probably the most courageous next step. We don't need more geniuses; we need more courageous people.[89]

—Charlie Gilkey

When have I let opportunities slip away while waiting for certainty?

Knowing that I'm usually better off making bold decisions, why *wouldn't* I go ahead with the decision I'm considering?

What might I regret at the end of my life?

Is what I most fear doing the thing I most need to do?

10

Always Free to Choose

Part of the reason we struggle to embrace no and say yes is that we're a little fuzzy in our understanding of what it is we're alive to do. What *is* the meaning of life?

A professor was lecturing to a philosophy class of mildly interested students. He said offhand, "You know, the meaning of life is easy—we are created to praise, glorify, and serve God, and by this means to achieve our eternal destiny!" This comment suddenly drew the interest of the students. They asked that he repeat what he had just said, word for word. The professor's comment came from the First Principle and Foundation at the beginning of St. Ignatius's *Spiritual Exercises*. It's right out of the *Catechism of the Catholic Church*. This is not exactly hidden knowledge. Still, this professor notes that his students "were fascinated at the idea that the meaning of life could be encapsulated in a handy sentence."[90]

I could not help but smile when I came across this story. I had similarly "discovered" the First Principle and Foundation when I was a freshman in college. I was amazed. I had found the meaning of life! Why had I never heard this before?

This idea may seem obvious to someone who grew up memorizing the Baltimore Catechism, but I didn't learn the catechism growing up. A significant part of my religious education was spent making felt banners and looking at religion textbooks filled with pictures. I had taken all sorts of AP courses, but my understanding of what we were here on this earth to do was rather elementary. Sadly, I'm not alone. The experience of learning many subjects but skipping over what's most important is all too common.

Life Happens. We're Still Free.

The year 2020 was a rough one. COVID-19 killed millions of people around the world. Many more lost their livelihoods because of the lockdowns and the contraction in the economy. Working parents were stretched thin. Some people started referring to it as the "worst year ever."

Not at all. Not even remotely close. Few people would want to trade places with someone in Europe in 1349, the worst year of the Black Death. That pandemic wiped out nearly half the continent. But the fourteenth century wasn't even the worst. Some historians have argued that if you're looking for the worst year in history, look no further than

AD 536.[91] That year, a volcanic eruption covered much of Europe and Asia in a sun-blocking fog for eighteen months. Temperatures dropped. Crops failed. People starved. And just to make things even more hellacious, there was also an outbreak of the bubonic plague. Oh, and they didn't have Zoom to connect with their loved ones and Netflix to stay entertained.

But humans are a resilient bunch. To people living through a difficult moment, it may seem that the sky is falling. People die. Those who live carry the scars of trauma. But, as a group, we keep rising. Babies are born. Communities are built. And people soon forget how much we have endured. Remarking on the persistence of humans, the author John Green writes, "I love dogged pursuits, and dogged efforts, and dogged determination. Now don't get me wrong—dogs are indeed very dogged. But they ought to call it humaned. Humaned determination."[92] If you look at the story of humanity, it's hard to argue with Green. We're pretty dogged—or humaned.

We do suffer. Even when we know that most people in history have had it much, much harder than we do, we still experience pain. Telling ourselves, "Well, at least it's not dysentery" does not help. It would be even worse if we tried to cheer up someone *else* by comparing their suffering with the suffering of others. I would be (even more of) a jerk if I went up to someone in pain and said, "Well, at least you're not a prisoner of war." No! Their suffering is real. People need to grieve.

Still, some perspective is helpful. The pain we are going through is real, but many people who have endured much worse have found that the pain was not the end of the story. *We* have probably gone through worse than what we are going through right now and found that it was not the end of the story. And we can choose how we will respond.

The Road to Power

I love looking at the lists of books that influenced people the most. One book often appears on the lists of people I admire: *Man's Search for Meaning* by Viktor Frankl. It's hard to have a pity party for yourself when you read about someone else enduring Nazi concentration camps. Everything was taken from Frankl—well, almost everything. He writes, "Everything can be taken from a man but one thing: the last of the human freedoms—to choose one's attitude in any given set of circumstances, to choose one's own way."[93]

Frankl watched as those around him gave up hope. He was constantly on the edge of death. But he talks about *freedom*.

No matter what happens to us, no matter what constraints are imposed, we control how we will respond to a situation.

The actor Will Smith expresses similar sentiments in an online video that went viral. Smith explains how he sees the difference between fault and responsibility. He says, "It's not your fault if your partner cheated and ruined your marriage. But it is for damn sure your responsibility to figure out how to take that pain and how to overcome that and build a happy life for yourself." Smith acknowledges that terrible things happen to us. That pain is real. Still, he argues that focusing on whose fault something is means that we are stuck in "victim mode." Instead, Smith argues, "The road to power is in taking responsibility."[94]

One can make good decisions and work hard and still face enormous challenges. Others can act irresponsibly but have it easy because of family privilege, a safety net, or the genetic lottery. There is much that is out of our control. But we can *always* do something about the problems that life throws our way. We cannot bring someone back to life or change what happened in the past. Our effort might only make a bad situation slightly less terrible. But we can take responsibility for doing the best we can with the hand we have been dealt.

Have To versus Get To

"I have to." "I get to." It's a word of difference, but when using one rather than the other in my internal monologue, it's often a world of difference.

I generally love school, except those times when I "have" to write a paper. On my better days, there are moments when I change my mental frame. Rather than "have" to write a paper, I try to think about how in this process I "get" to receive an education.

I still must write the paper, but it's a different experience. Rather than being pulled like an uncooperative donkey, "getting" to receive an education makes me feel grateful. Writing papers can even become enjoyable.

This "get to" mindset can work in many situations. When a housemate leaves an empty toilet-paper roll on the dispenser, I usually get frustrated about having to change it. I would be a much happier person if I saw it as an opportunity to get to do a simple service for others.

Not everything lends itself to this glass-half-full way of thinking. And I'm not going to tell someone *else*, "Wow, you get to deal with irritable bowel syndrome! That's awesome!" Still, the "get to" mindset can work more often than we might think. It's sad to attend funerals, for example, but we get to think about what this person has meant to us, show our support for the grieving, and confront death rather than run away from it.

I don't always practice this concept. I'm frustrated with traffic. I complain about how I "have to" go somewhere during rush hour rather than realize that I "get to" live in a dynamic place where people want to be.

Still, those better moments when I see how I "get to" do something reveal how *I have options*. I am always free to choose how to view what happens to me. Most important, I can choose how I am going to respond.

If we choose to be bitter and walk around with a chip on our shoulder because of everything we "have to" do, well, we will have plenty of company! That's a common choice. But it's not the only option. We can also reflect on all that we "get to" do, including the opportunity to push back against some of the bitterness of our world.

Commitments Are Not Stagnant

One of the things holding us back from making a commitment is the fear of boredom. Am I really going to do this type of work *for the rest of my life*? Am I going to be with the same person *every night*? That job or that person might be great, but *FOR-EV-ER*? (*The Sandlot*, anyone?)

For the first quarter of our lives, we're transitioning between different schools, friend groups, and hobbies every few years. The idea of doing anything for decades sounds like stagnation. When variety has marked our lives, sameness can appear utterly unattractive. Perhaps we fear turning into those people who still talk about the good old days—and still listen to the supposedly good music from those days. (It's even worse when they're referring to eighties music.)

But for one who dives into a commitment, "stagnant" is not an accurate description. The situation is usually much worse—and much better. A marriage involves the same partner, but that relationship is not the same through the years. Heartbreak is inevitable. The passion of the first few years will fade. There are bumps in the road—and sometimes crashes. In the middle of a relationship hurricane, "stagnant" might look appealing.

But when a relationship works, it *works*. The glow of newlyweds is unsustainable, but a different, deeper connection is possible. There's nothing quite like an older couple still in love after decades of daily commitment.

No commitment is static. Circumstances change. *We* change. Any commitment requires constant recommitment. Just because we have made an irreversible decision like marriage or religious vows does not mean we are finished. There is always more to discover about others and about ourselves. And then we recommit.

When I was discerning the priesthood, a priest mentor of mine shared with me that he lived a hand-to-mouth existence. Each day, he prayed for his daily bread to live another day faithfully. I was shocked. I saw him as a rock of a man. And he had to pray for strength each day? What about us mere mortals? But, of course, his strength lay precisely in the recognition of his weakness and the need for Someone else to fill his cup.

One might think, *Every day?* I have to ask God for help again and again? Does it never get easier? That's one view. Another way of seeing the same set of facts is to think, *Every day!* I "get to" rise back up and try again. Every day is a new adventure. There is always newness, even if those adventures are lived out within many of the same commitments.

What Is Your Current *Ikigai*?

Within one commitment we might pass through different "seasons." Having kids marks a significant change in a marriage. Managing teenagers is its own challenge. Living as empty nesters is yet another season in a married relationship.

It's common to hear a Jesuit say that the reasons he entered the Society of Jesus are not the same as the reasons he stays.

In looking back on a decision to join, he may realize that he was rather young and naive. The reality did not quite match his idealized picture. Still, that same Jesuit might notice that God continues to call him to this life—but as an imperfect sinner among fellow imperfect sinners.

Jesuits talk about finding one's "vocation within a vocation." One might have known that he was called to be a Jesuit brother, but through his formation process, he discovers a particular call to work with the marginalized. Or, one might have known for years that she was called to be a mom, but she discovers over time what her form of motherhood looks like. It could still be the same general commitment but now in high definition.

The Japanese have the concept of *ikigai*: "the reason you wake up in the morning." One's particular *ikigai* can change over the years. One might still seek to praise, reverence, and serve God, but the primary form of praise, reverence, and service can shift over time. What gets you up in the morning in your twenties likely is not going to be the same in your seventies. Life is not stagnant.

But Why Do We Have to Miss Out?

Stepping back, one could still ask, *But why do we do this?* Why do we have to commit—and miss out in the process?

Missing out is frustrating. Figuring out how best to commit is time consuming and nerve racking. Why do we have to do it? If God is love, why on earth does God make us go through this frustrating process?

This line of questioning touches on issues of free will and the problem of evil. Why do innocent children have to miss out? Why do people have to miss out because of tornadoes and infertility and pandemics? Believe me, I got questions! Questions that will not be answered this side of heaven. I need to accept that I'm going to "miss out" on some of the reasons for "missing out." Still, while recognizing that there will always be some element of mystery, we can explore these questions.

St. Ignatius's reasons for why we experience desolation can give some indications of why we miss out. As mentioned previously, Ignatius proposes three reasons for desolation. The first reason is that we are negligent. We're lazy and fail to pray. But negligence is not the only reason for desolation. Desolation can test us and teach us. Desolation also cultivates our humility and shows us that we are radically dependent upon God.

Missing out can work similarly. Much of the time, it's our own fault that we miss out. We play video games too much, our grades suffer, and we're rejected at the school of our choice. We meet the person of our dreams, but we never ask the person out. We don't get our act together and apply for the job in time. We don't move forward with our idea for a project because we're afraid it will fail.

But missing out is not always our fault. Taking responsibility, even when we were not the cause of our missing out, can teach us a lot. We would not grow as much as human persons without missing out and then rising above the disappointment. We may not *want* so many opportunities to grow. A simpler life can seem attractive. But that's usually not our choice. What we can choose to do is learn from the setbacks. And missing out, like desolation, teaches us to be humble. We cannot do things alone.

The Stoic philosopher Epictetus wrote, "When trouble comes, think of yourself as a wrestler whom God, like a trainer, has paired with a tough young buck. For what purpose? To turn you into Olympic-class material." But, Epictetus admits, "This is going to take some sweat to accomplish."[95] We would not develop into "Olympic-class" human beings—or just decent human beings—without missing out. We will never know what we are capable of without experiencing heartbreak and misfortune.

It's understandable to ask why God would allow us to miss out on so many things. I know I asked as a young child why

I had to miss out on having a dad to raise me. I can't pretend to tie things up in a neat and tidy bow. But our experience of missing out is inseparable from our own growth as human persons and our growth in relationship with our God. We have to miss out, but we get to grow.

We Still Have the Potential

You didn't honestly think that we were finished hearing from St. Ignatius, did you? Come on, now. I'm a Jesuit. We mention St. Ignatius of Loyola every chance we get. Do you realize how many schools and parishes are called "Ignatius" or "Loyola"?

I introduced part of the First Principle and Foundation at the beginning of this chapter. Even though that comes at the beginning of Ignatius's *Spiritual Exercises*, it's the perfect way to end this discussion of the freedom of missing out. According to Fr. David Fleming's contemporary translation of the First Principle and Foundation, Ignatius writes, "Everything has the potential of calling forth in us a more loving response to our life in God." No matter our circumstances, no matter the terrible commitments we've made in the past, we always have the freedom to choose that which leads to God's deepening life in us.

Even though you've missed out, you are in no less of a position to love. You can't lose! Sure, we can experience many losses along the way, but they don't have to be the end of the story. No matter what has happened in the past, right now, we are in no less of a position to love in the future.

We will face some disastrous situations. We *could* look at a dumpster fire and see only a dumpster fire. But we don't have to. We can also see the opportunity to grow from such a situation—to see how we are people who can endure even terrible situations! It's the best practical joke you can play on Life or the Evil Spirit or whatever jerk you want to call out by name who caused such a dumpster fire. You might say, "You think you're bringing me down? Well, with grace, I'm going to use this experience to grow." Things will often get better—and if not, well, you'll have more of an opportunity to continue growing! In every situation, even the crummy ones, we have the chance to move forward.

If Viktor Frankl can talk about freedom while watching people all around him die in Nazi concentration camps, then we, too, can talk about freedom. No matter what has happened, no matter how many mistakes we have made, right now we are in no less of a position to love. We are free to choose. So, how will we respond?

What Can I Do Now?

The goal of our life is to live with God forever. God, who loves us, gave us life. Our own response of love allows God's life to flow into us without limit. All the things in this world are gifts from God, presented to us so that we can know God more easily and make a return of love more readily. As a result, we appreciate and use all these gifts of God insofar as they help us to develop as loving persons. But if any of these gifts become the center of our lives, they displace God and so hinder our growth toward our goal.

In everyday life, then, we must hold ourselves in balance before all of these created gifts insofar as we have a choice and are not bound by some obligation. We should not fix our desires on health or sickness, wealth or poverty, success or failure, a long life or a short one. For everything has the potential of calling forth in us a deeper response to our life in God.

Our only desire and our one choice should be this: I want and I choose what better leads to God's deepening his life in me.

—Contemporary translation of the First Principle and Foundation by David Fleming, SJ

Continued

What is my personal First Principle and Foundation? What am I on this earth to do?

How focused am I on whose fault something is? How can I better focus on my own responsibility to move forward?

How can I flip something I "have to" do into something I "get to" do?

What's my current *ikigai*, my reason to wake up in the morning?

Endnotes

1. Viktor Frankl, *Man's Search for Meaning* (Boston, Mass.: Beacon Press, 2014), 150.

2. David Brooks, *The Second Mountain: The Quest for a Moral Life* (New York: Random House, 2019), 20.

3. David Brooks, *The Road to Character* (New York: Random House, 2016), xi.

4. https://www.cnbc.com/2017/10/04/students-who-work-actually-get-better-grades-but-theres-a-catch.html.

5. G. K. Chesterton, *The Three Apologies of G. K. Chesterton: Heretics, Orthodoxy & The Everlasting Man* (Bristol, U.K.: Mockingbird Press, 2018), 245.

6. Mark Manson, *The Subtle Art of Not Giving a F*ck: A Counterintuitive Approach to Living a Good Life* (New York: HarperCollins, 2016), 166.

7. Thomas Hobbes, *Leviathan* (Ottawa, Ontario, Canada: East India Publishing Company, 2021).

8. Sheena Iyengar and Mark R. Lepper, "When Choice Is Demotivating: Can One Desire Too Much of a Good Thing?" *Journal of Personality and Social Psychology* 79, no. 6 (2000): 995,

https://faculty.washington.edu/jdb/345/345%20Articles/
Iyengar%20%26%20Lepper%20(2000).pdf.

9. Nathaniel Meyersohn, "How a Cheap, Brutally Efficient Grocery
   Chain Is Upending America's Supermarkets," CNN, May 17, 2019,
   https://edition.cnn.com/interactive/2019/05/business/
   aldi-walmart-low-food-prices/index.html.

10. https://www.theguardian.com/lifeandstyle/2015/oct/21/
    choice-stressing-us-out-dating-partners-monopolies.

11. https: //www.inc.com/marcel-schwantes/
    warren-buffet-says-this-career-advice-is-all-wrong-its-like-saving-up-
    sex-for-your-old-age-it-just-doesnt-make-a-lot-of-sense.html

12. https://www.thecrimson.com/article/2017/5/25/
    desai-commencement-ed/.

13. Ibid.

14. Barry Schwartz, *The Paradox of Choice* (New York: HarperCollins,
    2004, 2016), 145f.

15. https://www.usccb.org/topics/marriage-and-family-life-ministries/
    when-i-call-help-pastoral-response-domestic-violence.

16. https://www.ted.com/talks/
    dan_gilbert_the_surprising_science_of_happiness?language=en.

17. C. S. Lewis, *The Four Loves* (Orlando, Fla.: Harcourt, Brace, and
    Company, 1960, 1988), 121.

18. https://www.inc.com/robert-glazer/
    every-entrepreneur-should-hear-this-message-warren-buffett-gave-hi
    s-pilot-about-setting-goals.html.

19. https://www.forbes.com/sites/amyblaschka/2019/11/26/
    this-is-why-saying-no-is-the-best-way-to-grow-your-career-and-how
    -to-do-it/.

20. https://www.forbes.com/sites/carminegallo/2011/05/16/
    steve-jobs-get-rid-of-the-crappy-stuff/?sh=327e18cb7145.

21. https://www.nytimes.com/2014/09/11/fashion/
    steve-jobs-apple-was-a-low-tech-parent.html

22. Angela Duckworth, *Grit* (New York: Scribner, 2016).

23. Morten Hansen, *Great at Work: The Hidden Habits of Top Performers*
    (New York: Simon and Schuster, 2018), 37.

24. "So You Want to Play Pro Basketball" https://www.nytimes.com/
    interactive/2013/11/03/sunday-review/
    so-you-want-to-play-pro-basketball.html.

25. https://www.ted.com/talks/
    dan_gilbert_the_surprising_science_of_happiness/
    transcript?language=en.

26. Francis Cardinal George, O.M.I., *God in Action: How Faith in God
    Can Address the Challenges of the World* (New York: Doubleday
    Religion, 2011), 88.

27. Jacques Philippe, *Interior Freedom* (New York: Scepter Publishers,
    Inc, 2007), 28.

28. Rich Karlgaard, *Late Bloomers: The Hidden Strengths of Learning and
    Succeeding at Your Own Pace* (New York: Broadway Books,
    2019), 163.

29. https://seths.blog/2019/08/streaks/.

30. https://sive.rs/hyn.

31. Brené Brown, PhD, LMSW, *The Gifts of Imperfection: Let Go of Who You Think You're Supposed to Be and Embrace Who You Are* (Center City, Minn: Hazelden, 2010), xiii.

32. Francis, *Evangelii Gaudium*, 6, https://www.vatican.va/content/ francesco/en/apost_exhortations/documents/ papa-francesco_esortazione-ap_20131124_evangelii-gaudium.html.

33. Ibid., 10.

34. https://quoteinvestigator.com/2020/08/17/face/.

35. Jordan B. Peterson, *Beyond Order: 12 More Rules for Life* (New York: Portfolio/Penguin, 2021), 385.

36. Malcolm Gladwell, *David and Goliath* (New York: Little, Brown and Company, 2013).

37. David Brooks, "How to Survive the Blitz," *The Atlantic* (March 29, 2020), https://www.theatlantic.com/ideas/archive/2020/03/ virus-and-blitz/608965/.

38. https://www.cambridge.org/core/journals/ the-british-journal-of-psychiatry/article/ effect-of-11-september-2001-terrorist-attacks-in-the-usa-on-suicide-in-areas-surrounding-the-crash-sites/ F4AF49A4F85B791060EF8AF8DA70EEEB.

39. Jorge Luis Borges, *Twenty-Four Conversations with Borges: Interviews by Roberto Alifano 1981–1983* (New York: Grove Press/Atlantic, 1984).

40. Aleksandr Solzhenitsyn, *The Gulag Archipelago 1918–1956*, trans. Thomas P. Whitney and Harry Willetts; abr. by Edward E. Ericson Jr. (New York: Perennial, 1983), 313.

41. https://www.vatican.va/content/francesco/en/encyclicals/documents/ papa-francesco_20201003_enciclica-fratelli-tutti.html, 78.

42. Leonard Cohen, "Anthem," https://www.youtube.com/ watch?v=c8-BT6y_wYg.

43. Edmund Burke, *Reflections on the Revolution in France and Other Writings* (New York: Everyman's Library/Alfred A. Knopf, 1910, 2015), 365.

44. Paul Chrystal, *The Ancient Greeks in 100 Facts* (Gloucestershire, United Kingdom: Amberley Publishing, 2017), chapter 81.

45. https://www.instagram.com/p/Bve-c82g1ni/?hl=en.

46. Pierre Teilhard de Chardin, "Patient Trust" (poem).

47. https://www.nytimes.com/1998/11/12/technology/ to-a-haiku-writer-spam-is-poetry-in-a-can.html.

48. https://www.villagevoice.com/2009/09/25/ our-10-best-spam-haikus/.

49. Greg Lukianoff and Jonathan Haidt, *The Coddling of the American Mind: How Good Intentions and Bad Ideas Are Setting Up a Generation for Failure* (New York: Penguin Press, 2018).

50. For those who aren't from Nebraska or Iowa, let me explain. Workers—oftentimes students—remove the tassels from corn so that the plants can cross-fertilize. It's hard work and a rite of passage

for many Midwestern teenagers. Walking beans is the hand weeding of soybeans. It's less common today because of herbicides.

51. Edmund Burke, "A Letter from Mr. Burke to a Member of the National Assembly in Answer to Some Objections to His Book on French Affairs," 3rd ed. (London, 1791), 69.

52. Bob Sullivan, "Memo to Work Martyrs: Long Hours Make You Less Productive," January 26, 2015, https://www.cnbc.com/2015/01/26/working-more-than-50-hours-makes-you-less-productive.html.

53. Howard V. Hong and Edna H. Hong, eds. *The Essential Kierkegaard* (Princeton, N.J.: Princeton University Press, 1978, 1980), 502.

54. Malcolm Gladwell, *Outliers* (New York: Little, Brown and Company, 2008).

55. Alex Soojung-Kim Pang, *Rest: Why You Get More Done When You Work Less* (New York: Basic Books/Hachette Book Group, 2016).

56. https://www.themarginalian.org/2014/01/16/kurt-vonnegut-joe-heller-having-enough/.

57. Robert D. Putnam, *Bowling Alone: The Collapse and Revival of American Community* (New York: Simon and Schuster, 2001).

58. Francis, *Evangelii Gaudium*, 270.

59. https://www.nytimes.com/2021/05/07/opinion/motherhood-baby-bust-early-parenthood.html.

60. Erik Barker, *Barking Up the Wrong Tree: The Surprising Science Behind Why Everything You Know about Success Is (Mostly) Wrong* (New York: HarperCollins, 2017), 243.

61. Ariston Anderson, "On the Creative Process and Getting Your Work Noticed," 99u.Adobe.com (blog), November 20, 2012, https://99u.adobe.com/articles/7252/ tim-ferriss-on-the-creative-process-and-getting-your-work-noticed.

62. Olga Khazan, "Just Eat More Fiber," *The Atlantic*, January 9, 2019, https://www.theatlantic.com/health/archive/2018/01/ just-eat-more-fiber/550082/.

63. James Clear, "Why Trying to Be Perfect Won't Help You Achieve Your Goals (And What Will)," excerpt from *Atomic Habits*, https://jamesclear.com/repetitions.

64. Adam Grant, *Originals: How Non-Conformists Move the World* (New York: Penguin, 2017), 36.

65. Chris Baty, *No Plot? No Problem! A Low-stress, High-velocity Guide to Writing a Novel in 30 Days* (San Francisco: Chronicle Books, 2004, 2014), 33.

66. Tina Fey, *Bossypants* (New York: Little, Brown and Company, 2011), 123.

67. Elizabeth Gilbert, *Big Magic: Creative Living beyond Fear* (New York: Riverhead/Penguin Random House, 2015), 25.

68. https://paulmitchell.blog/2021/07/27/forgiving-reality/.

69. Marcus Aurelius, *Meditations*, trans. Martin Hammond (UK, Penguin/Random House, 2014), 6.13, 67.

70. Kevin Enochs, "In US, Interpolitical Marriage Increasingly Frowned Upon," VOA News, February 3, 2017, https://www.voanews.com/ a/mixed-political-marriages-an-issue-on-rise/3705468.html.

71. Fyodor Dostoevsky, *The Brothers Karamazov*, trans. Richard Pevear and Larissa Volokhonsky (New York: Farrar, Straus and Giroux, 1990), 56.

72. *Catechism of the Catholic Church*, 1733.

73. Martin Seligman, *Flourish* (New York: Free Press/Simon and Schuster, 2011), 20.

74. Rod Dreher, *Live Not by Lies* (New York: Sentinel/Penguin Random House, 2020), 152.

75. Gordon Livingstone, MD, *Too Soon Old, Too Late Smart* (Philadelphia: Da Capo Press, 2004), 152.

76. Brendan Comerford, *The Pilgrim's Story* (Chicago: Loyola Press, 2021), 69.

77. Daniel Asa Rose, Interview with Ann Lamott, Lit Hub.com, November 9, 2018, https://lithub.com/radical-hope-and-laughter-an-interview-with-anne-lamott/.

78. Ross Douthat, "The Case for One More Child: Why Large Families Will Save Humanity," *Plough Quarterly*, November 8, 2020, https://www.plough.com/en/topics/life/parenting/the-case-for-one-more-child.

79. Sebastian Junger, *Tribe: On Homecoming and Belonging* (New York: Hachette Book Group, 2016), xvii.

80. Rodney Stark and William Sims Bainbridge, *A Theory of Religion* (New Brunswick, N.J.: Rutgers University Press, 1996), 125.

81. Fr. James Mallon, *Divine Renovation: Bringing Your Parish from Maintenance to Mission* (Toronto, Canada: Novalis Publishing, 2014), Kindle Location 2245.

82. Ryan Holiday, "If You're Not Seeking Out Challenges, How Are You Going to Get Better?" (blog) July 14, 2020, https://ryanholiday.net/seek-challenge/.

83. Steven D. Levitt, *Heads or Tails: The Impact of a Coin Toss on Major Life Decisions and Subsequent Happiness* (working paper), https://www.nber.org/system/files/working_papers/w22487/w22487.pdf.

84. Claude S. Fischer, "The Great Settling Down," https://aeon.co/essays/the-increasingly-mobile-us-is-a-myth-that-needs-to-move-on.

85. Taylor Locke, "At Age 30, Jeff Bezos Thought This Would Be His One Big Regret in Life," January 18, 2020, https://www.cnbc.com/2020/01/17/at-age-30-jeff-bezos-thought-this-would-be-his-one-big-regret-in-life.html.

86. https://www.aboutamazon.com/news/company-news/2016-letter-to-shareholders.

87. Bronnie Ware, *Regrets of the Dying* (blog), https://bronnieware.com/blog/regrets-of-the-dying/.

88. https://news.stanford.edu/2005/06/14/jobs-061505/.

89. Charlie Gilkey, *Start Finishing: How to Go from Idea to Done* (Boulder, Colo.: Sounds True Publishing, 2019), 32.

90. Timothy P. Muldoon, "Why Young Adults Need Ignatian Spirituality," *America* (February 26, 2001).

91. Becky Little, "The Worst Time in History to Be Alive, According to Science," https://www.history.com/news/536-volcanic-eruption-fog-eclipse-worst-year.

92. John Green, "Humanity's Temporal Range," The Anthropocene Reviewed (podcast) New York Public Radio, March 26, 2020, https://www.wnycstudios.org/podcasts/anthropocene-reviewed/episodes/anthropocene-reviewed-humanitys-temporal-range.

93. Viktor E. Frankl, *Man's Search for Meaning*, trans. Ilse Lasch (Boston, Mass.: Beacon Press, 1959), 75.

94. https://www.youtube.com/watch?v=Ln21-WhJyec.

95. https://stoic-quotes.online/quotes/a-stoic-quote-by-epictetus-from-discourses-i-241-2_4eab7/.

About the Author

Rev. Michael Rossmann, SJ, is a Jesuit priest and doctoral student at the Gregorian University in Rome. He previously served as the editor-in-chief of The *Jesuit Post*, where he started the popular video series "One-Minute Homily." He continues to produce short-but-substantive videos for social media. He is a native of Iowa City and a graduate of the University of Notre Dame.